Jessica Gherri

Logicals für den Englischunterricht

Rätsel für die 7./8. Klasse in zwei Differenzierungsstufen

Jessica Gherri unterrichtet Englisch an der Grund- und Mittelstufe in Berlin.

Wir verwenden in unseren Werken eine genderneutrale Sprache, damit sich alle gleichermaßen angesprochen fühlen. Wenn keine neutrale Formulierung möglich ist, nennen wir die weibliche und die männliche Form. In Fällen, in denen wir aufgrund einer besseren Lesbarkeit nur ein Geschlecht nennen können, achten wir darauf, den unterschiedlichen Geschlechtsidentitäten gleichermaßen gerecht zu werden.

In diesem Werk sind nach dem MarkenG geschützte Marken und sonstige Kennzeichen für eine bessere Lesbarkeit nicht besonders kenntlich gemacht. Es kann also aus dem Fehlen eines entsprechenden Hinweises nicht geschlossen werden, dass es sich um einen freien Warennamen handelt.

4. Auflage 2025

AAP Lehrerwelt GmbH
Veritaskai 3
21079 Hamburg
Telefon: +49 (0) 40325083-040
E-Mail: info@lehrerwelt.de
Geschäftsführung: Andrea Fischer, Sandra Saghbazarian
USt-ID: DE 173 77 61 42
Register: AG Hamburg HRB/126335

Autorschaft: Jessica Gherri
Covergestaltung: TSA&B Werbeagentur GmbH, Hamburg
Illustrationen: Kerrin Paulsen, Stefan Lucas, Julia Flasche, Barbara Gerth, Fides Friedeberg, Oliver Wetterauer, Natalie Meenen, Manuela Ostadal, Bert Breitenbach, Marion El-Khalafawi, Katharina Reichert-Scarborough
Satz: Satzpunkt Ursula Ewert GmbH, Bayreuth
Druck und Bindung: PMLS GmbH & Co. KG, Kassel

ISBN/Bestellnummer: 978-3-403-23643-6
www.persen.de

Inhalt

Vorwort

Liebe Kolleginnen und Kollegen,

dieser dritte Logical Band richtet sich an den Englischunterricht in den Klassen 7 und 8. Die beliebten Logicals machen den Kindern viel Spaß. Sie lesen, knobeln, kombinieren und lösen die Frage zu jedem Logical. Thematisch richten sich die Logicals nach den Anforderungen der Rahmenlehrpläne und fördern die Lesekompetenz der Schülerinnen und Schüler.

Die Logicals bieten Ihnen als Fachlehrkraft oder auch als fachfremd Unterrichtende zahlreiche Einsatzmöglichkeiten:

- zur Vertiefung und Wiederholung von Unterrichtsthemen
- zur Differenzierung
- als Einstieg in ein Unterrichtsthema
- als Hausaufgabe
- im Frontalunterricht
- in der Stationsarbeit
- in der Freiarbeit
- in der Wochenplanarbeit
- als Vertretungsstunde
- in der Partner- oder Gruppenarbeit (auch als Schnelligkeitswettkampf)
- als Hörverstehensaufgabe, wenn Sie die Anweisungen in der (evtl. richtigen) Reihenfolge diktieren und den Kindern lediglich die Tabelle oder das Bild vorlegen.

Die in jedem Logical enthaltene Frage, wird durch sorgfältiges Lesen beantwortet. Denn nur wer genau liest, die Informationen kombiniert und mitdenkt, kommt zur Lösung. Auf diesem Weg lernen die Kinder systematisch vorzugehen, sich zu konzentrieren und Spaß am Denken und Verstehenden Lesen zu haben. Der Einsatz der Logicals fördert also die Lesefähigkeit und Denkfähigkeit. Die Kinder fühlen sich als kleine Detektive und haben schnell Erfolgserlebnisse. Die verschiedenen Schwierigkeitsstufen der Logicals werden den unterschiedlichen Fähigkeiten jedes Kindes gerecht und ermöglichen die erforderliche Differenzierung.

Jedes Thema beinhaltet zwei Schwierigkeitsstufen:

easy ( ) besteht aus 11 Sätzen und **more difficult** ( ) aus 13 Sätzen.

Je mehr gelesen werden muss, desto mehr muss kombiniert und mitgedacht werden, denn sowohl die Fülle an Informationen als auch die Anforderungen der Satzstrukturen (Negativsätze, Konditional, Relativsätze, *simple present*, *simple past*) nehmen zu. So können Sie die Logicals zur Leistungsdifferenzierung verwenden (ggf. kann der erste Lösungssatz vorgegeben werden).

Eine **Neuerung** ist, dass Logicals zu einem Thema eine **gemeinsame Frage** haben, die beantwortet werden muss. So soll sichergestellt werden, dass alle Kinder an dem gleichen Thema auf unterschiedlichen Niveaus arbeiten, aber zu dem gleichen Ergebnis kommen.

Falls den Kindern die Übungsform der Logicals noch unbekannt sein sollte, empfiehlt es sich, zuvor ein deutschsprachiges Logical gemeinsam in der Klasse zu bearbeiten (siehe Kapitel „Beispiel eines einfachen Logicals in Tabellenform"). Sätze aus denen Informationen verarbeitet wurden, können abgehakt werden. Dies erleichtert die Übersicht. Wenn die Logicals in der Freiarbeit eingesetzt werden und die Kinder zur Kontrolle Einsicht in die Lösung erhalten, fördert dies zusätzlich das selbstständige Arbeiten.

Die Logicals beinhalten unterschiedliche Herangehensweisen. So sollen in vielen Logicals **Tabellen** ausgefüllt ( ) werden. Es gibt aber auch Logicals, die durch **Ausmalen** ( ) von Bildern oder durch **selbstständiges Zeichnen** ( ) zu lösen sind. Die Herangehensweise ist dem alphabetisch sortierten Inhaltsverzeichnis zu entnehmen, ebenso wie die wichtigsten in den Logicals verwendeten **Vokabeln/Begriffe** sowie **grammatische Hinweise**.

Ich wünsche Ihnen und Ihren Schülerinnen und Schülern viel Spaß beim Lösen!
Jessica Gherri

Beispiel für ein einfaches Logical in Tabellenform

Basketballspieler tragen unterschiedliche Kleidung, je nachdem zu welchem Verein sie gehören. Außerdem sind sie ziemlich groß.
Lies, fülle die Tabelle aus und finde heraus:

Welcher Spieler ist 2,11 m groß? ______________________

Spieler	1	2	3	4	5
Körpergröße					
Farbe des Tops					
Farbe der Shorts					
Farbe des Balls					

1. Ein Spieler hat einen orangefarbenen Ball und schwarze Shorts.
2. Der Spieler mit gelben Shorts und grünem Ball ist neben dem Spieler mit roten Shorts.
3. Ein Spieler hat ein grünes Top und ist 2,06 m groß.
4. Der 1,96 m große Spieler steht nicht neben dem 1,98 m großen Spieler.
5. Der Spieler rechts hat einen gelben Ball und rote Shorts.
6. Der Spieler mit dem gelben Top ist zwischen dem Spieler mit dem braunen Top und dem Spieler mit dem blauen Top.
7. Zwischen dem 2,06 m großen Spieler und dem 1,98 m großen Spieler ist ein 2,14 m großer Spieler.
8. Neben dem Spieler mit gelben Shorts ist ein Spieler mit lilafarbenen Shorts und blauem Ball.
9. Links neben dem Spieler mit dem braunen Top ist ein Spieler mit rotem Top.
10. Der Spieler mit dem roten Ball hat ein braunes Top.
11. Der Spieler mit den blauen Shorts ist neben dem Spieler mit dem blauen Ball.

Lösung: Spieler 2
Mögliche Satzreihenfolge: 5/2/8/11/1/10/9/6/3/7/4

Spieler	1	2	3	4	5
Körpergröße	1,96 m	**2,11 m**	1,98 m	2,14 m	2,06 m
Farbe des Tops	rot	braun	gelb	blau	grün
Farbe der Shorts	schwarz	blau	lila	gelb	rot
Farbe des Balls	orange	rot	blau	grün	gelb

Übersichtstabelle

 ausmalen  Tabelle ausfüllen  selbst zeichnen

	Work Sheets	Vocabulary			
			easy		more difficult
1	**Aliens**		arms, legs, eyes, mouths, noses, ears		arms, legs, eyes, mouths, noses, ears
2	**At the beach**		swimsuit/swimming trunks, parasol, deckchair, swimming goggles, snorkel		swimsuit/swimming trunks, parasol, deckchair, swimming goggles, snorkel
3	**At the supermarket** (relative clauses)		fruit, apples, bananas, oranges, pineapples, cereals, cornflakes, muesli, Crunchy Nuts, Smacks, chocolate, chewing gums, lollipops, liquorice, toast, sliced bread, croissants, bread rolls, milk, water, cola light, cocoa		**additionally:** raspberries, minced meat pie, Weetabix, jelly beans, orange juice
4	**British Kings and Queens** (simple past, relative clauses)		Henry VIII, Queen Victoria, Richard the Lionheart, William the Conquerer, Elizabeth I, wives, illegitimate, age, reigned, married, children, 3rd Crusade		**additionally:** Mary I, Bloody Mary
5	**Buckingham Palace**		State Dining Room, Blue Drawing Room, Music Room, White Drawing Room, Royal Closet, Private Apartments, East Gallery, Green Drawing Room, Throne Room, Yellow Drawing Room, Balcony Room, Chinese Luncheon Room, The Quadrangle		**additionally:** Service Areas, Ball Room, Cross Gallery
6	**Communication** (relative clauses)		contacts, communicate, sister, girlfriend, dad, boyfriend, mum, brother, best friend, e-mail, letter, postcard, mobile phone, Facebook, Twitter, text message		**additionally:** Facebook, four friends
7	**Crimes at school** (simple past, relative clauses)		secretary, headmistress, pupil, Maths teacher, caretaker, key, folder, guitar, iPad, pencil case, jacket, thumbprint, footprints, coke tin, DNA, brown hair, scrap of cloth		**additionally:** pupil, pencil case, handbag, fingerprints
8	**Detectives** (simple past, relative clauses)		criminal case, months, Adrian Monk, Miss Marple, Sherlock Holmes, Hercule Poirot, Famous Five, The Three Investigators, murder, blackmail, kidnapping, burglary, robbery, fraud		**additionally:** year
9	**Favourite jobs** (conditional + negative)		country, nurse, teacher,doctor, hair stylist, writer, librarian, cook, secretary, zoo keeper, architect		**additionally:** football player, dentist
10	**Favourite teachers** (relative clauses)		likes, dislikes, favourite, teachers, German, Physical Education, Geography, Music, English, Art, Biology, Maths, Chemistry, Spanish, French		**additionally:** History, Religious Education
11	**Flowers**		vase, roses, tulips, lily, gerbera, pinks		vase, roses, tulips, lily, gerbera, pinks
12	**Football kits**		football, football socks, football kit, trainers		football, football socks, football kit, trainers
13	**Hobbies** (relative clauses)		months, making music, reading books, meeting friends, riding a horse, taking photos, chatting on Facebook, listening to CDs, playing online games, collecting autographs, playing Wii U		**additionally:** painting, playing the guitar
14	**Jobs at home** (like + gerund)		days of the week, ironing, taking out the rubbish, making breakfast, making the beds, cooking, washing the dishes, laying the table, walking the dog, going shopping, washing the dishes		**additionally:** vacuum cleaning the flat, watering the plants

Übersichtstabelle

 ausmalen

 Tabelle ausfüllen

 selbst zeichnen

	Work Sheets	Vocabulary			
			easy		more difficult
15	**Laying the table**		knives, forks, spoons, glasses, paper napkins, plates		knives, forks, spoons, glasses, paper napkins, plates
16	**London** (3rd person -s, relative clauses)		days, boat, tube, bus, on foot, taxi, Tower of London, Speaker's Corner, Piccadilly Circus, Houses of Parliament, Greenwich		**additionally:** bike, London Eye
17	**Paintings**		geometric shapes, circle, triangle, rectangle, square		geometric shapes, circle, triangle, rectangle, square
18	**Parrots**		head, beak, body, wings, tail		head, beak, body, wings, tail
19	**Pizzas** (3rd person -s, relative clauses)		orange juice, sprite, cola light, apple juice, Fanta, topping, salami, mushrooms, ham, pineapple, broccoli, rocket, red pepper, olives, shrimps		**additionally:** cola, tuna, onions
20	**Pocket money** (3rd person -s, relative clauses)		piggy bank, daily, weekly, monthly, every two weeks, every three weeks, £		**additionally:** every ten days
21	**Shopping summer clothes** (3rd person -s, relative clauses)		T-shirt, trousers, jeans, skirt, shoes		T-shirt, trousers, jeans, skirt, shoes
22	**Shopping winter clothes**		anorak, trousers, boots, scarf, woolly hat		anorak, trousers, boots, scarf, woolly hat
23	**Sights in the USA** (3rd person -s, relative clauses)		months,Florida, California, Nevada, South Dakota, New York, Walt Disney World Resort, Golden Gate Bridge, Las Vegas, Mount Rushmore National Memorial, Empire State Building		**additionally:** Arizona, Grand Canyon
24	**Sports** (likes/dislikes + gerund, relative clauses)		training, days, likes, dislikes, gymnastics, playing volleyball, cycling, playing table tennis, playing football, athletics, swimming, playing tennis, dancing, playing badminton		**additionally:** playing basketball, playing golf
25	**US Presidents** (simple past, relative clauses)		party, republican, democrat, presidential period, special information, age, George Washington, Abraham Lincoln, Ronald Reagan, John F. Kennedy, first president, abolished slavery, made cowboy films, was shot in Dallas		**additionally:** Franklin D. Roosevelt, more than two presidential periods

Aliens

Aliens from outer space look differently to what we call a body. Here you can see some alien bodies, but their arms, legs, eyes, mouths, noses and ears are missing. Read, complete the aliens and find out:

Which alien has four ears? ______________

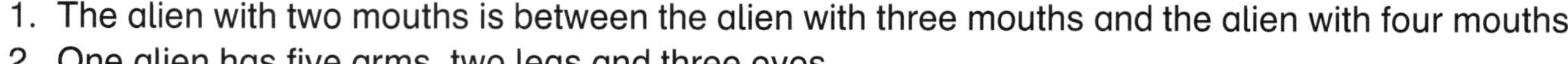

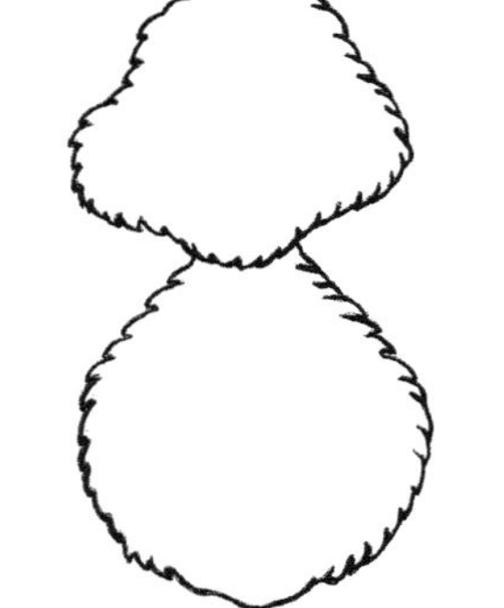

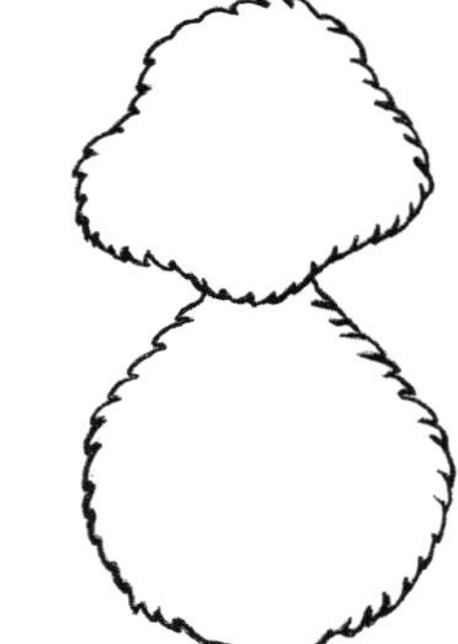

Alien 1 **Alien 2** **Alien 3** **Alien 4**

1. The alien with two mouths is between the alien with three mouths and the alien with four mouths.
2. One alien has five arms, two legs and three eyes.
3. The alien with one nose is between the alien with three noses and the alien with five noses.
4. The alien with six ears is not next to the one with three ears.
5. The alien on the left has two arms.
6. One alien has four eyes, five legs and three mouths.
7. Next to the alien with three eyes is an alien with five eyes and three legs.
8. One alien has two noses and three ears.
9. Next to the alien with five eyes is an alien with one eye and six legs.
10. The alien with four arms is between the alien with two arms and the one with six arms.
11. One alien has five mouths, three noses and five ears.

Aliens

Aliens from outer space look differently to what we call a body. Here you can see some alien bodies, but their arms, legs, eyes, mouths, noses and ears are missing. Read, complete the aliens and find out:

Which alien has four ears? ______________

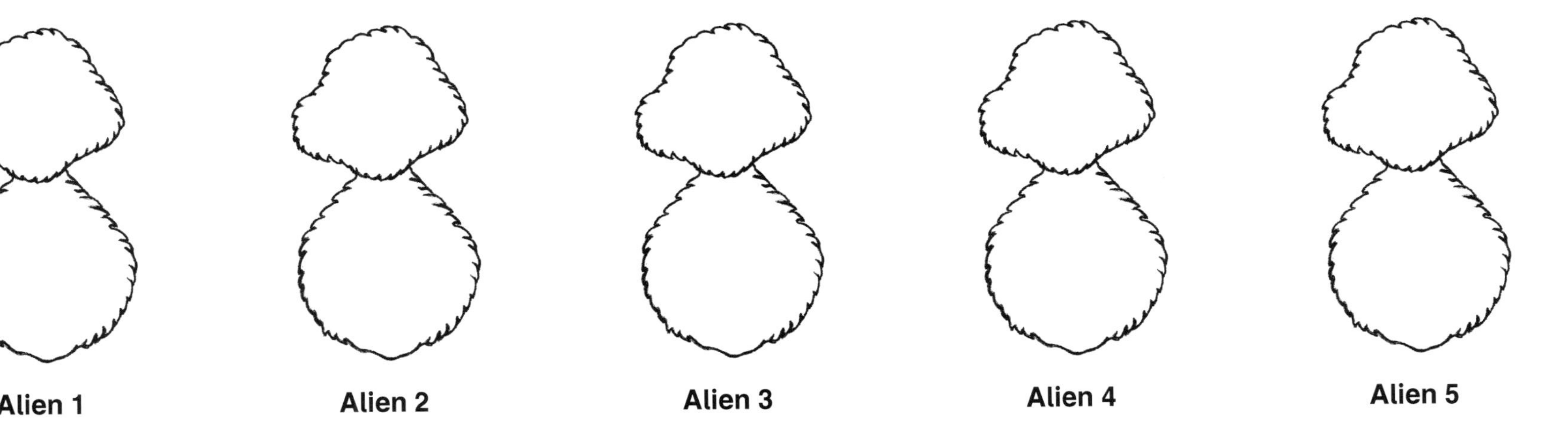

1. The alien with five ears is between the alien with one ear and the one with six ears.
2. One alien has one arm, four legs and six eyes.
3. One alien has four eyes, three mouths and two noses.
4. One alien has one mouth, six noses and one ear.
5. The alien on the left has two arms.
6. The alien with two mouths and five noses is between the one with two noses and the one with four mouths and one nose.
7. Next to the alien with three eyes is an alien with three legs and five eyes.
8. The alien with three ears is not next to the alien with six ears.
9. The alien with six legs and one eye is between the alien with five eyes and the one with five legs.
10. The alien with four arms is between the alien with two arms and the one with six arms.
11. Next to the alien with one nose is an alien with five mouths and three noses.
12. Next to the alien with six eyes is an alien with three eyes.
13. Next to the alien with six arms is an alien with five arms and two legs.

Aliens

Aliens from outer space look differently to what we call a body. Here you can see some alien bodies, but their arms, legs, eyes, mouths, noses and ears are missing. Read, complete the aliens and find out:

Which alien has four ears? **Alien 2**
Possible solution: 5/10/2/7/9/6/1/11/3/8/4

	Alien 1	Alien 2	Alien 3	Alien 4
arms	2	4	6	5
legs	5	6	3	2
eyes	4	1	5	3
mouths	3	2	4	5
noses	2	5	1	3
ears	3	**4**	6	5

5. The alien on the left has two arms.
10. The alien with four arms is between the alien with two arms and the one with six arms.
2. One alien has five arms, two legs and three eyes.
7. Next to the alien with three eyes is an alien with five eyes and three legs.
9. Next to the alien with five eyes is an alien with one eye and six legs.
6. One alien has four eyes, five legs and three mouths.
1. The alien with two mouths is between the alien with three mouths and the alien with four mouths.
11. One alien has five mouths, three noses and five ears.
3. The alien with one nose is between the alien with three noses and the alien with five noses.
8. One alien has two noses and three ears.
4. The alien with six ears is not next to the one with three ears.

Aliens

Aliens from outer space look differently to what we call a body. Here you can see some alien bodies, but their arms, legs, eyes, mouths, noses and ears are missing. Read, complete the aliens and find out:

Which alien has four ears? **Alien 2**
Possible solution: 5/10/13/2/12/7/9/3/6/11/4/1/8

	Alien 1	Alien 2	Alien 3	Alien 4	Alien 5
arms	2	4	6	5	1
legs	5	6	3	2	4
eyes	4	1	5	3	6
mouths	3	2	4	5	1
noses	2	5	1	3	6
ears	3	**4**	6	5	1

5. The alien on the left has two arms.
10. The alien with four arms is between the alien with two arms and the one with six arms.
13. Next to the alien with six arms is an alien with five arms and two legs.
2. One alien has one arm, four legs and six eyes.
12. Next to the alien with six eyes is an alien with three eyes.
7. Next to the alien with three eyes is an alien with three legs and five eyes.
9. The alien with six legs and one eye is between the alien with five eyes and the one with five legs.
3. One alien has four eyes, three mouths and two noses.
6. The alien with two mouths and five noses is between the one with two noses and the one with four mouths and one nose.
11. Next to the alien with one nose is an alien with five mouths and three noses.
4. One alien has one mouth, six noses and one ear.
1. The alien with five ears is between the alien with one ear and the one with six ears.
8. The alien with three ears is not next to the alien with six ears.

At the beach

Summer holidays are here and children go to the beach whenever it is possible. They lie on deckchairs under parasols. They have swimming goggles and snorkels with them. Read, colour and find out:

Who has a yellow snorkel? ______________________

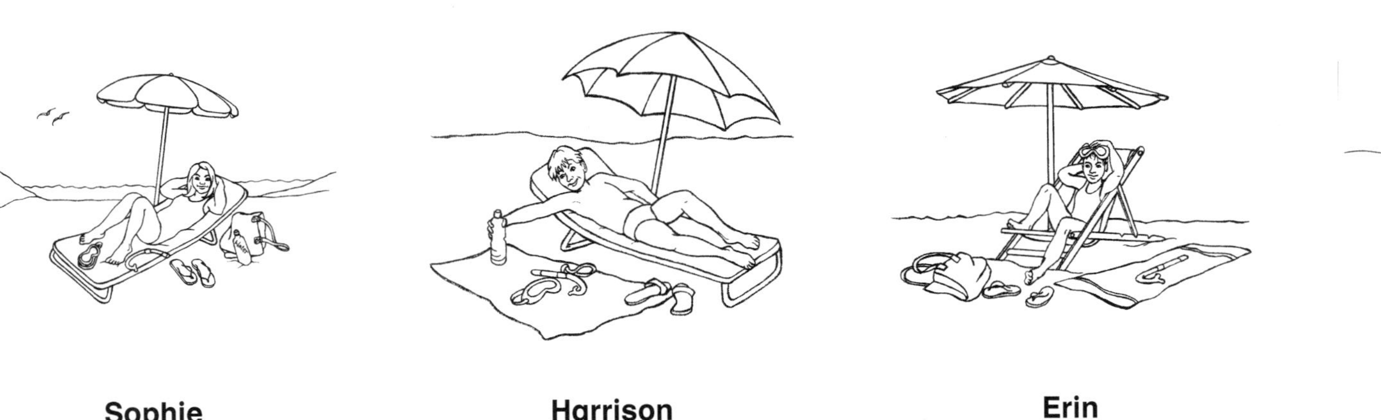

1. The blue parasol is between the purple and the yellow parasol.
2. The green deckchair is between the blue and the red deckchair.
3. The girl on the left has a green swimsuit and next to her is a boy with blue swimming trunks.
4. One boy has red swimming goggles.
5. One child lies under a red parasol on a blue deckchair.
6. Between the child with the orange snorkel and the one with the green snorkel is a child with a pink snorkel.
7. Next to the boy with the blue swimming trunks is a girl with an orange swimsuit.
8. The child with the yellow swimming goggles is next to the one with the blue swimming goggles.
9. One child has black swimming trunks and lies under a purple parasol.
10. One child has purple swimming goggles and an orange snorkel.
11. One child lies on an orange deckchair and has blue swimming goggles.

At the beach

Summer holidays are here and children go to the beach whenever it is possible. They lie on deckchairs under parasols. They have swimming goggles and snorkels with them. Read, colour and find out:

Who has a yellow snorkel? ______________

Sophie **Harrison** **Erin** **Luke** **Layla**

1. Next to the blue parasol is a yellow parasol.
2. One child lies on a purple deckchair and has orange swimming goggles and a red snorkel.
3. The child on the left has a green swimsuit and next to her is a boy with blue swimming trunks.
4. One child has a yellow swimsuit and lies under a green parasol.
5. The child with the red swimming goggles is next to the one with the yellow swimming goggles.
6. One child lies under a red parasol on a blue deckchair.
7. Between the child with the blue swimming trunks and the one with black swimming trunks is a child with an orange swimsuit.
8. The child with the blue swimming goggles is between the one with the orange swimming goggles and the one with the yellow swimming goggles.
9. The green deckchair is between the blue and the red deckchair.
10. One child has purple swimming goggles and an orange snorkel.
11. The purple parasol is between the green and the blue parasol.
12. The orange deckchair is next to the red deckchair.
13. Between the child with the orange snorkel and the one with the green snorkel is a child with a pink snorkel.

Lösungen

At the beach

Summer holidays are here and children go to the beach whenever it is possible. They lie on deckchairs under parasols. They have swimming goggles and snorkels with them. Read, colour and find out:

Who has a yellow snorkel? **Luke**
Possible solution: 3/7/9/1/5/2/11/8/4/10/6

	Sophie	Harrison	Erin	Luke
swimsuit/swimming trunks	green	blue	orange	black
parasol	red	yellow	blue	purple
deckchair	blue	green	red	orange
swimming goggles	purple	red	yellow	blue
snorkel	orange	pink	green	**yellow**

3. The girl on the left has a green swimsuit and next to her is a boy with blue swimming trunks.
7. Next to the boy with the blue swimming trunks is a girl with an orange swimsuit.
9. One child has black swimming trunks and lies under a purple parasol.
1. The blue parasol is between the purple and the yellow parasol.
5. One child lies under a red parasol on a blue deckchair.
2. The green deckchair is between the blue and the red deckchair.
11. One child lies on an orange deckchair and has blue swimming goggles.
8. The child with the yellow swimming goggles is next to the one with the blue swimming goggles.
4. One boy has red swimming goggles.
10. One child has purple swimming goggles and an orange snorkel.
6. Between the child with the orange snorkel and the one with the green snorkel

At the beach

Summer holidays are here and children go to the beach whenever it is possible. They lie on deckchairs under parasols. They have swimming goggles and snorkels with them. Read, colour and find out:

Who has a yellow snorkel? **Luke**
Possible solution: 3/7/4/11/1/6/9/12/2/8/5/10/13

	Sophie	Harrison	Erin	Luke	Layla
swimsuit/swimming trunks	green	blue	orange	black	yellow
parasol	red	yellow	blue	purple	green
deckchair	blue	green	red	orange	purple
swimming goggles	purple	red	yellow	blue	orange
snorkel	orange	pink	green	**yellow**	red

3. The child on the left has a green swimsuit and next to her is a boy with blue swimming trunks.
7. Between the child with the blue swimming trunks and the one with black swimming trunks is a child with an orange swimsuit.
4. One child has a yellow swimsuit and lies under a green parasol.
11. The purple parasol is between the green and the blue parasol.
1. Next to the blue parasol is a yellow parasol.
6. One child lies under a red parasol on a blue deckchair.
9. The green deckchair is between the blue and the red deckchair.
12. The orange deckchair is next to the red deckchair.
2. One child lies on a purple deckchair and has orange swimming goggles and a red snorkel.
8. The child with the blue swimming goggles is between the one with the orange swimming goggles and the one with the yellow swimming goggles.
5. The child with the red swimming goggles is next to the one with the yellow swimming goggles.
10. One child has purple swimming goggles and an orange snorkel.
13. Between the child with the orange snorkel and the one with the green snorkel is a child with a pink snorkel.

At the supermarket

Some teenagers go shopping at a supermarket. They fill their shopping trolleys with fruit, cereals, sweets, bread and something to drink. Read, fill in the table and find out:

Who buys cocoa? ____________________

name	Leroy	Pamela	Scarlett	Anthony
fruit				
cereal product				
bread				
sweets				
drink				

1. Between the teenager who buys chocolate and the one who buys lollipops is a teenager who buys chewing gum.
2. Leroy buys apples and crispy flakes.
3. Next to the teenager who buys bread rolls is a teenager who buys croissants.
4. Next to the teenager who buys apples is a teenager who buys bananas and honey flakes.
5. The teenager who buys water is next to the one who buys apple juice.
6. One teenager buys pineapples, nut flakes and bread rolls.
7. One teenager buys liquorice and apple juice.
8. One girl buys sliced bread.
9. The teenager who buys oranges and muesli is next to the one who buys bananas.
10. One boy buys milk.
11. One teenager buys toast and chocolate.

At the supermarket

Some teenagers go shopping at a supermarket. They fill their shopping trolleys with fruit, cereals, sweets, bread and something to drink. Read, fill in the table and find out:

Who buys cocoa? ____________________

name	Leroy	Pamela	Scarlett	Anthony	Pete
fruit					
cereal product					
bread					
sweets					
drink					

1. Between the teenager who buys a minced meat pie and the one who buys croissants is a teenager who buys bread rolls.
2. One teenager buys toast and chocolate.
3. One boy buys milk.
4. The teenager who buys liquorice is next to the one that buys lollipops.
5. Next to the teenager who buys oranges is a teenager who buys pineapples and nut flakes.
6. Leroy buys apples and crispy flakes.
7. The teenager who buys water is next to the one who buys apple juice.
8. One teenager buys raspberries, chocolate muesli and a minced meat pie.
9. One teenager buys a marzipan bar and orange juice.
10. Between the teenager who buys apples and the one that buys oranges and muesli is a teenager who buys bananas and honey flakes.
11. Next to the teenager who buys croissants is a teenager who buys sliced bread.
12. The teenager who buys apple juice is next to the one who buys orange juice.
13. Between the teenager who buys chocolate and the one who buys lollipops is a teenager who buys chewing gums.

At the supermarket

Some teenagers go shopping at a supermarket. They fill their shopping trolleys with fruit, cereals, sweets, bread and something to drink. Read, fill in the table and find out:

Who buys cocoa? **Pamela**
Possible solution: 2/4/9/6/3/8/11/1/7/5/10

name	Leroy	Pamela	Scarlett	Anthony
fruit	apples	bananas	oranges	pineapples
cereal product	crispy flakes	honey flakes	muesli	nut flakes
bread	toast	sliced bread	croissants	bread rolls
sweets	chocolate	chewing gum	lollipops	liquorice
drink	milk	**cocoa**	water	apple juice

2. Leroy buys apples and crispy flakes.
4. Next to the teenager who buys apples is a teenager who buys bananas and honey flakes.
9. The teenager who buys oranges and muesli is next to the one who buys bananas.
6. One teenager buys pineapples, nut flakes and bread rolls.
3. Next to the teenager who buys bread rolls is a teenager who buys croissants.
8. One girl buys sliced bread.
11. One teenager buys toast and chocolate.
1. Between the teenager who buys chocolate and the one who buys lollipops is a teenager who buys chewing gum.
7. One teenager buys liquorice and apple juice.
5. The teenager who buys water is next to the one who buys apple juice.
10. One boy buys milk.

At the supermarket

Some teenagers go shopping at a supermarket. They fill their shopping trolleys with fruit, cereals, sweets, bread and something to drink. Read, fill in the table and find out:

Who buys cocoa? **Pamela**
Possible solution: 6/10/5/8/1/11/2/13/4/9/12/7/3

name	Leroy	Pamela	Scarlett	Anthony	Pete
fruit	apples	bananas	oranges	pineapples	raspberries
cereal product	crispy flakes	honey flakes	muesli	nut flakes	chocolate muesli
bread	toast	sliced bread	croissants	bread rolls	minced meat pie
sweets	chocolate	chewing gum	lollipops	liquorice	a marzipan bar
drink	milk	**cocoa**	water	apple juice	orange juice

6. Leroy buys apples and crispy flakes.
10. Between the teenager who buys apples and the one that buys oranges and muesli is a teenager who buys bananas and honey flakes.
5. Next to the teenager who buys oranges is a teenager who buys pineapples and nut flakes.
8. One teenager buys raspberries, chocolate muesli and a minced meat pie.
1. Between the teenager who buys a minced meat pie and the one who buys croissants is a teenager who buys bread rolls.
11. Next to the teenager who buys croissants is a teenager who buys sliced bread.
2. One teenager buys toast and chocolate.
13. Between the teenager who buys chocolate and the one who buys lollipops is a teenager who buys chewing gums.
4. The teenager who buys liquorice is next to the one that buys lollipops.
9. One teenager buys a marzipan bar and orange juice.
12. The teenager who buys apple juice is next to the one who buys orange juice.
7. The teenager who buys water is next to the one who buys apple juice.
3. One boy buys milk.

British Kings and Queens

There were a lot of famous Kings and Queens in Britain. They always reigned until they died.
Did you know that one of them built the Tower of London?
Read the sentences, fill in the table and find out:

Who had nine children and married a German? It was ______________________

King/Queen					
age					
reigned					
children and special information					

1. The King who became 59 years old is between the one who became 70 and the one who became 42 years old.
2. Henry VIII is on the left and next to him is Queen Victoria.
3. The Queen who reigned from 1837–1901 is between the one who died in 1547 and the one who reigned from 1189–1199.
4. Between the Queen who never married and the King who had no children and fought in the third Crusade is the King who built the Tower of London and who had ten children.
5. The Queen who became 82 years old is next to the one who became 42 years old.
6. Between Queen Victoria and William the Conqueror is Richard the Lionheart.
7. The King who reigned from 1066–1087 is next to the one who died in 1199.
8. One King became 56 years old and reigned from 1509–1547.
9. Elizabeth I became 70 years old.
10. The Queen who reigned from 1558–1603 had no children and never married.
11. The King who had six wives and an illegitimate daughter (Queen Elizabeth I) is not next to the King who fought in the third Crusade.

British Kings and Queens

There were a lot of famous Kings and Queens in Britain. They always reigned until they died.
Did you know that one of them built the Tower of London?
Read the sentences, fill in the table and find out:

Who had nine children and married a German? It was ________________

King/Queen						
age						
reigned						
children and special information						

1. William the Conqueror is between Richard the Lionheart and Elizabeth I.
2. Henry VIII is on the left.
3. The Queen who reigned from 1837–1901 is between the King who died in 1547 and the one who reigned from 1189–1199.
4. Between the Queen who had no children and the King who built the Tower of London and had ten children is a Queen who never married and had no children.
5. Between Henry VIII and Richard the Lionheart is Queen Victoria.
6. Next to the King who had ten children is a King who had no children and fought in the third Crusade.
7. The Queen who became 70 years old is between the one who became 42 years old and the one who became 59 years old.
8. One King had six wives and an illegitimate daughter – Queen Elizabeth I.
9. Between the King who died in 1199 and the Queen who reigned from 1558–1603 is a King who reigned from 1066–1087.
10. The King who became 56 years old reigned from 1509–1547.
11. The Queen who reigned from 1553–1558 had no children and was called Bloody Mary.
12. The King who became also only 42 years old is between the one who became 59 and the one who became 82 years old.
13. Mary I became 42 years old.

Lösungen

British Kings and Queens

There were a lot of famous Kings and Queens in Britain. They always reigned until they died. Did you know that one of them built the Tower of London? Read the sentences, fill in the table and find out:

Who had nine children and married a German? It was **Queen Victoria**
Possible solution: 2/6/9/1/5/8/3/7/10/4/11

King/Queen	Henry VIII	**Queen Victoria**	Richard the Lionheart	William the Conqueror	Elizabeth I
age	56 years old	82 years old	42 years old	59 years old	70 years old
reigned	1509–1547	1837–1901	1189–1199	1066–1087	1558–1603
children and special information	had 6 wives and an illegitimate daughter Queen Elizabeth I	**married a German Prince and had 9 children**	had no children and fought in the 3rd Crusade	had 10 children and built the Tower of London	had no children and never married

2. Henry VIII is on the left and next to him is Queen Victoria.
6. Between Queen Victoria and William the Conqueror is Richard the Lionheart.
9. Elizabeth I became 70 years old.
1. The King who became 59 years old is between the one who became 70 and the one who became 42 years old.
5. The Queen who became 82 years old is next to the one who became 42 years old.
8. One King became 56 years old and reigned from 1509–1547.
3. The Queen who reigned from 1837–1901 is between the one who died in 1547 and the one who reigned from 1189–1199.
7. The King who reigned from 1066–1087 is next to the one who died in 1199.
10. The Queen who reigned from 1558–1603 had no children and never married.
4. Between the Queen who never married and the King who had no children and fought in the third Crusade is the King who built the Tower of London and who had ten children.
11. The King who had six wives and an illegitimate daughter (Queen Elizabeth I) is not next to the King who fought in the third Crusade.

British Kings and Queens

There were a lot of famous Kings and Queens in Britain. They always reigned until they died. Did you know that one of them built the Tower of London? Read the sentences, fill in the table and find out:

Who had nine children and married a German? It was **Queen Victoria**
Possible solution: 2/5/1/13/7/12/10/3/9/11/4/6/8

King/Queen	Henry VIII	**Queen Victoria**	Richard the Lionheart	William the Conqueror	Elizabeth I	Mary I
age	56 years old	82 years old	42 years old	59 years old	70 years old	42 years old
reigned	1509–1547	1837–1901	1189–1199	1066–1087	1558–1603	1553–1558
children and special information	had 6 wives and an illegitimate daughter (Queen Elizabeth I)	**married a German Prince and had 9 children**	had no children and fought in the 3rd Crusade	had 10 children and built the Tower of London	had no children and never married	had no children and was called Bloody Mary

2. Henry VIII is on the left.
5. Between Henry VIII and Richard the Lionheart is Queen Victoria.
1. William the Conqueror is between Richard the Lionheart and Elizabeth I.
13. Mary I became 42 years old.
7. The Queen who became 70 years old is between the one who became 42 years old and the one who became 59 years old.
12. The King who became also only 42 years old is between the one who became 59 and the one who became 82 years old.
10. The King who became 56 years old reigned from 1509–1547.
3. The Queen who reigned from 1837–1901 is between the King who died in 1547 and the one who reigned from 1189–1199.
9. Between the King who died in 1199 and the Queen who reigned from 1558–1603 is a King who reigned from 1066–1087.
11. The Queen who reigned from 1553–1558 had no children and was called Bloody Mary.
4. Between the Queen who had no children and the King who built the Tower of London and had ten children is a Queen who never married and had no children.
6. Next to the King who had ten children is a King who had no children and fought in the third Crusade.
8. One King had six wives and an illegitimate daughter – Queen Elizabeth I.

Buckingham Palace

Buckingham Palace was built in 1703. Queen Victoria used it as official residence in London since 1837. Nowadays tourists can visit some of the rooms in August and September every year. When the Queen is in London you can see the Union Jack on top of the roof. This plan of Buckingham Palace is very simplified.

Read, name the rooms and find out: Which room is the Throne Room?

____

1. The centre of Buckingham Palace is called The Quadrangle.
2. Next to the Royal Closet is the White Drawing Room.
3. One room in the East is the Chinese Luncheon Room.
4. Next to the Blue Drawing Room is the State Dining Room.
5. Opposite the Private Apartments on the right is the Royal Closet.
6. The biggest room in the East is the famous Balcony Room.
7. Go along the corridors from the Chinese Luncheon Room and you will find the bigger Private Apartments on the right.
8. Next to the East Gallery is the Green Drawing Room.
9. Between the White Drawing Room and the Blue Drawing Room is the protruding Music Room.
10. On the left of the Balcony room is the Yellow Drawing Room.
11. Opposite the State Dining Room is the long East Gallery.

1 Service Areas
2 Ball Room
3 Cross Gallery
4 __________
5 __________
6 __________
7 __________
8 __________
9 __________
10 __________
11 __________
12 __________
13 __________
14 __________
15 __________
16 __________

Buckingham Palace

Buckingham Palace was built in 1703. Queen Victoria used it as official residence in London since 1837. Nowadays tourists can visit some of the rooms in August and September every year. When the Queen is in London you can see the Union Jack on top of the roof. This plan of Buckingham Palace is very simplified.

Read, name the rooms and find out: Which room is the Throne Room?

____

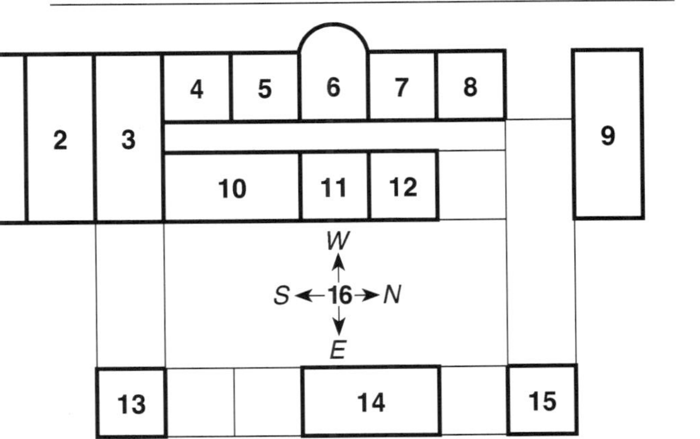

1. The centre of Buckingham Palace is called The Quadrangle.
2. Go along the corridors from the Chinese Luncheon Room and you will find the bigger Private Apartments on the right.
3. Between the White Drawing Room and the Blue Drawing Room is the protruding Music Room.
4. The Ball Room is between the Cross Gallery and the Service Areas.
5. One big room is the East Gallery.
6. The biggest room in the East is the famous Balcony Room.
7. Next to the Blue Drawing Room is the State Dining Room.
8. One room in the East is the Chinese Luncheon Room.
9. Next to the Royal Closet is the White Drawing Room.
10. On the left of the Balcony Room is the Yellow Drawing Room.
11. The Cross Gallery is next to the State Dining Room.
12. Next to the East Gallery is the Green Drawing Room.
13. Opposite the Private Apartments on the right is the Royal Closet.

Buckingham Palace

Buckingham Palace was built in 1703. Queen Victoria used it as official residence in London since 1837. Nowadays tourists can visit some of the rooms in August and September every year. When the Queen is in London you can see the Union Jack on top of the roof. This plan of Buckingham Palace is very simplified.

Read, name the rooms and find out: Which room is the Throne Room?
Room number 12

Possible solution: 1/6/10/3/7/5/2/9/4/11/8

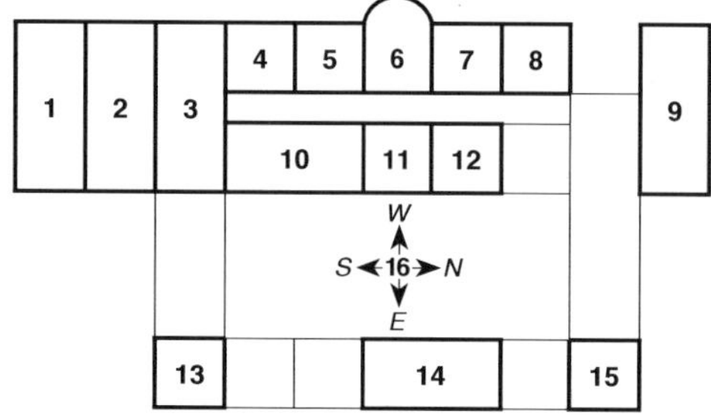

1 Service Areas	7 White Drawing Room	13 Yellow Drawing Room
2 Ball Room	8 Royal Closet	14 Balcony Room
3 Cross Gallery	9 Private Apartments	15 Chinese Luncheon Room
4 State Dining Room	10 East Gallery	16 The Quadrangle
5 Blue Drawing Room	11 Green Drawing Room	
6 Music Room	**12 Throne Room**	

1. The centre of Buckingham Palace is called The Quadrangle.
6. The biggest room in the East is the famous Balcony Room.
10. On the left of the Balcony room is the Yellow Drawing Room.
3. One room in the East is the Chinese Luncheon Room.
7. Go along the corridors from the Chinese Luncheon Room and you will find the bigger Private Apartments on the right.
5. Opposite the Private Apartments on the right is the Royal Closet.
2. Next to the Royal Closet is the White Drawing Room.
9. Between the White Drawing Room and the Blue Drawing Room is the protruding Music Room.
4. Next to the Blue Drawing Room is the State Dining Room.
11. Opposite the State Dining Room is the long East Gallery.
8. Next to the East Gallery is the Green Drawing Room.

Buckingham Palace

Buckingham Palace was built in 1703. Queen Victoria used it as official residence in London since 1837. Nowadays tourists can visit some of the rooms in August and September every year. When the Queen is in London you can see the Union Jack on top of the roof. This plan of Buckingham Palace is very simplified.

Read, name the rooms and find out: Which room is the Throne Room?
Room number 12

Possible solution: 1/6/10/8/2/13/9/3/7/11/4/5/12

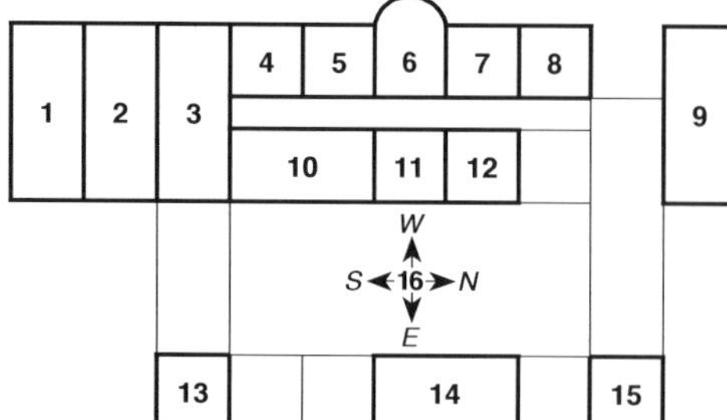

1 Service Areas	7 White Drawing Room	13 Yellow Drawing Room
2 Ball Room	8 Royal Closet	14 Balcony Room
3 Cross Gallery	9 Private Apartments	15 Chinese Luncheon Room
4 State Dining Room	10 East Gallery	16 The Quadrangle
5 Blue Drawing Room	11 Green Drawing Room	
6 Music Room	**12 Throne Room**	

1. The centre of Buckingham Palace is called The Quadrangle.
6. The biggest room in the East is the famous Balcony Room.
10. On the left of the Balcony Room is the Yellow Drawing Room.
8. One room in the East is the Chinese Luncheon Room.
2. Go along the corridors from the Chinese Luncheon Room and you will find the bigger Private Apartments on the right.
13. Opposite the Private Apartments on the right is the Royal Closet.
9. Next to the Royal Closet is the White Drawing Room.
3. Between the White Drawing Room and the Blue Drawing Room is the protruding Music Room.
7. Next to the Blue Drawing Room is the State Dining Room.
11. The Cross Gallery is next to the State Dining Room.
4. The Ball Room is between the Cross Gallery and the Service Areas.
5. One big room is the East Gallery.
12. Next to the East Gallery is the Green Drawing Room.

Communication

People nowadays keep in contact by various means. Among young people mobile phones and computers are very popular.
Look at these children.
Read, fill in the table and find out:

Who communicates by What's App? ______________

name							
contact person							
communication							

1. The child who contacts his brother is between the child who contacts her best friend and the one who contacts her mum.
2. Emily is between Jacob and Chloe.
3. The child who communicates via mobile phone is between the one who sends a text message and the one who sends a letter.
4. The child who contacts her boyfriend is between the one who contacts her mum and the one who contacts his dad.
5. The child on the left is Sophia.
6. The child who contacts his girlfriend is between the one who contacts his dad and the one who contacts her sister via e-mail.
7. Next to the child who sends a letter is a child who communicates by Twitter.
8. Isla contacts her best friend.
9. Henry is between Sophia and Jacob.
10. The child who sends a postcard is between the child who sends an e-mail and the one who sends a text message.
11. Samuel is next to Chloe.

Communication

People nowadays keep in contact by various means. Among young people mobile phones and computers are very popular.
Look at these children.
Read, fill in the table and find out:

Who communicates by What's App? ______________

name								
contact person								
communication								

1. Oscar is between Jacob and Emily.
2. The child who contacts his dad is between the child who contacts four friends and the one who contacts his girlfriend.
3. The child on the left is Sophia.
4. The child who communicates via Facebook is between the one who sends a text message and the one who communicates by mobile phone.
5. Next to the child who sends a letter is a child who communicates by Twitter.
6. The child who contacts her boyfriend is between the one who contacts four friends and the one who contacts her mum.
7. Henry is between Sophia and Jacob.
8. The child who contacts his brother is between the one who contacts her best friend and the one who contacts her mum.
9. One child contacts her sister via e-mail.
10. Chloe is between Emily and Samuel.
11. Next to the child who communicates by mobile phone is a child who sends a letter.
12. Isla contacts her best friend.
13. The child who sends a postcard is between the child who sends an e-mail and the one who sends a text message.

Communication

People nowadays keep in contact by various means. Among young people mobile phones and computers are very popular.
Look at these children.
Read, fill in the table and find out:

Who communicates by What's App? **Isla**
Possible solution: 5/9/2/11/8/1/4/6/10/3/7

name	Sophia	Henry	Jacob	Emily	Chloe	Samuel	**Isla**
contact person	sister	girlfriend	dad	boyfriend	mum	brother	best friend
communication	e-mail	postcard	text message	mobile phone	letter	Twitter	**What's App**

5. The child on the left is Sophia.
9. Henry is between Sophia and Jacob.
2. Emily is between Jacob and Chloe.
11. Samuel is next to Chloe.
8. Isla contacts her best friend.
1. The child who contacts his brother is between the child who contacts her best friend and the one who contacts her mum.
4. The child who contacts her boyfriend is between the one who contacts her mum and the one who contacts his dad.
6. The child who contacts his girlfriend is between the one who contacts his dad and the one who contacts her sister via e-mail.
10. The child who sends a postcard is between the child who sends an e-mail and the one who sends a text message.
3. The child who communicates via mobile phone is between the one who sends a text message and the one who sends a letter.
7. Next to the child who sends a letter is a child who communicates by Twitter.

Communication

People nowadays keep in contact by various means. Among young people mobile phones and computers are very popular.
Look at these children.
Read, fill in the table and find out:

Who communicates by What's App? **Isla**
Possible solution: 3/7/1/10/12/8/6/2/9/13/4/11/5

name	Sophia	Henry	Jacob	Oscar	Emily	Chloe	Samuel	**Isla**
contact person	sister	girlfriend	dad	four friends	boyfriend	mum	brother	best friend
communication	e-mail	postcard	text message	Facebook	mobile phone	letter	Twitter	**What's App**

3. The child on the left is Sophia.
7. Henry is between Sophia and Jacob.
1. Oscar is between Jacob and Emily.
10. Chloe is between Emily and Samuel.
12. Isla contacts her best friend.
8. The child who contacts his brother is between the one who contacts her best friend and the one who contacts her mum.
6. The child who contacts her boyfriend is between the one who contacts four friends and the one who contacts her mum.
2. The child who contacts his dad is between the child who contacts four friends and the one who contacts his girlfriend.
9. One child contacts her sister via e-mail.
13. The child who sends a postcard is between the child who sends an e-mail and the one who sends a text message.
4. The child who communicates via Facebook is between the one who sends a text message and the one who communicates by mobile phone.
11. Next to the child who communicates by mobile phone is a child who sends a letter.
5. Next to the child who sends a letter is a child who communicates by Twitter.

Crimes at school

Here are five suspects. They all stole something from the staff room at school. But they left traces at the crime scene that help the detectives find out exactly who stole what. Read, fill in the table and find out:

Who left a thumbprint at the crime scene? ______________________

suspect					
stolen item					
stolen item					
trace					

1. Next to the person who stole a laptop is a person who stole a pencil case.
2. Next to the Maths teacher is the headmistress.
3. One person stole a jacket and a scarf and left footprints at the crime scene.
4. The person who left a glass with DNA is not next to the person who left a scrap of cloth at the crime scene.
5. The person on the right is the trainee.
6. The caretaker stole a schoolbag.
7. One person stole a key and left a scrap of cloth at the crime scene.
8. The pupil is between the trainee and the Maths teacher.
9. Between the person who stole a schoolbag and the one who stole a laptop is a person who stole a folder.
10. Between the person who stole the handbag and the one who stole a pencil is a person who stole a purse.
11. Next to the person who left footprints at the crime scene is a person who stole a handbag and left fingerprints.

Crimes at school

Here are six suspects. They all stole something from the staff room at school. But they left traces at the crime scene that help the detectives find out exactly who stole what. Read, fill in the table and find out:

Who left a thumbprint at the crime scene? ____________________

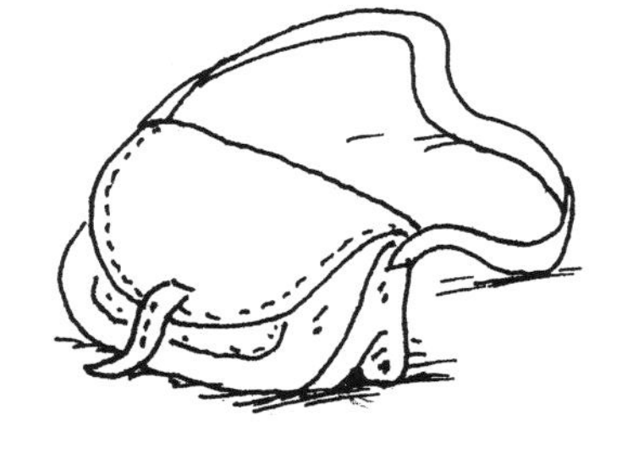

suspect						
stolen item						
stolen item						
trace						

1. Between the person who stole a schoolbag and the one who stole a guitar is a person who stole a folder.
2. Next to the person who left footprints at the crime scene is a person who stole a handbag.
3. The person who stole a key and left a scrap of cloth at the crime scene is not next to the person who stole a mobile phone.
4. Between the Maths teacher and the headmistress is the secretary.
5. The person who stole a laptop is between the person who stole a guitar and the person who stole a pencil case.
6. The person on the right is the trainee.
7. Between the person who stole the handbag and the one who stole a mobile phone is a person who stole a purse.
8. One person stole a jacket and a scarf and left footprints at the crime scene.
9. The caretaker stole a schoolbag.
10. On the right next to the person who left a brown hair at the crime scene is a person who left a glass with DNA.
11. The pupil is between the trainee and the Maths teacher.
12. Next to the person who left a glass with DNA at the crime scene is a person who left fingerprints.
13. The person who stole a pencil is next to the person who left a brown hair at the crime scene.

Crimes at school

Here are six suspects. They all stole something from the staff room at school. But they left traces at the crime scene that help the detectives find out exactly who stole what. Read, fill in the table and find out:

Who left a thumbprint? **The headmistress**
Possible solution: 5/8/2/6/9/1/3/11/10/7/4

suspect	caretaker	**headmistress**	Maths teacher	pupil	trainee
stolen item	schoolbag	folder	laptop	pencil case	jacket
stolen item	key	pencil	purse	handbag	scarf
trace	scrap of cloth	**thumbprint**	glass with DNA	fingerprints	footprints

5. The person on the right is the trainee.
8. The pupil is between the trainee and the Maths teacher.
2. Next to the Maths teacher is the headmistress.
6. The caretaker stole a schoolbag.
9. Between the person who stole a schoolbag and the one who stole a laptop is a person who stole a folder.
1. Next to the person who stole a laptop is a person who stole a pencil case.
3. One person stole a jacket and a scarf and left footprints at the crime scene.
11. Next to the person who left footprints at the crime scene is a person who stole a handbag and left fingerprints.
10. Between the person who stole the handbag and the one who stole a pencil is a person who stole a purse.
7. One person stole a key and left a scrap of cloth at the crime scene.
4. The person who left a glass with DNA is not next to the person who left a scrap of cloth at the crime scene.

Crimes at school

Here are six suspects. They all stole something from the staff room at school. But they left traces at the crime scene that help the detectives find out exactly who stole what. Read, fill in the table and find out:

Who left a thumbprint at the crime scene? **The headmistress**
Possible solution: 6/11/4/9/1/5/8/2/7/3/13/10/12

suspect	caretaker	**headmistress**	secretary	Maths teacher	pupil	trainee
stolen item	schoolbag	folder	guitar	laptop	pencil case	jacket
stolen item	key	pencil	mobile phone	purse	handbag	scarf
trace	scrap of cloth	**thumbprint**	brown hair	glass with DNA	fingerprints	footprints

6. The person on the right is the trainee.
11. The pupil is between the trainee and the Maths teacher.
4. Between the Maths teacher and the headmistress is the secretary.
9. The caretaker stole a schoolbag.
1. Between the person who stole a schoolbag and the one who stole a guitar is a person who stole a folder.
5. The person who stole a laptop is between the person who stole a guitar and the person who stole a pencil case.
8. One person stole a jacket and a scarf and left footprints at the crime scene.
2. Next to the person who left footprints at the crime scene is a person who stole a handbag.
7. Between the person who stole the handbag and the one who stole a mobile phone is a person who stole a purse.
3. The person who stole a key and left a scrap of cloth at the crime scene is not next to the person who stole a mobile phone.
13. The person who stole a pencil is next to the person who left a brown hair at the crime scene.
10. On the right next to the person who left a brown hair at the crime scene is a person who left a glass with DNA.
12. Next to the person who left a glass with DNA at the crime scene is a person who left fingerprints.

Detectives

Children are fascinated by crime stories. This child collects books about famous detectives.
In each book a detective solved a criminal case in a specific month.
Read, fill in the table and find out:

Who solved a robbery? ____________________

detective						
month						
criminal case						

1. The detective who solved a criminal case in November is not next to the detective who solved a criminal case in December.
2. A book about Miss Marple is on the left.
3. The detective who solved a blackmail is between the detectives who solved a kidnapping and the detective who solved a burglary.
4. Adrian Monk solved a criminal case in September.
5. Between the book about the Famous Five and the book about The Three Investigators is a book about Sherlock Holmes.
6. The detective who solved a murder is between the detectives who solved a fraud and the detectives who solved a kidnapping.
7. The detectives who solved a criminal case in January are between the detective who solved a criminal case in June and the detective who solved a criminal case in December.
8. Next to the book about Miss Marple is a book about the Famous Five.
9. The fraud was solved in May.
10. Next to the detective who solved a criminal case in September is a detective who solved a criminal case in June.
11. The book about Hercule Poirot is next to the book about The Three Investigators.

Detectives

Children are fascinated by crime stories. This child collects books about famous detectives. In each book a detective solved a criminal case in a specific month and year. Read, fill in the table and find out:

Who solved a robbery? ____________

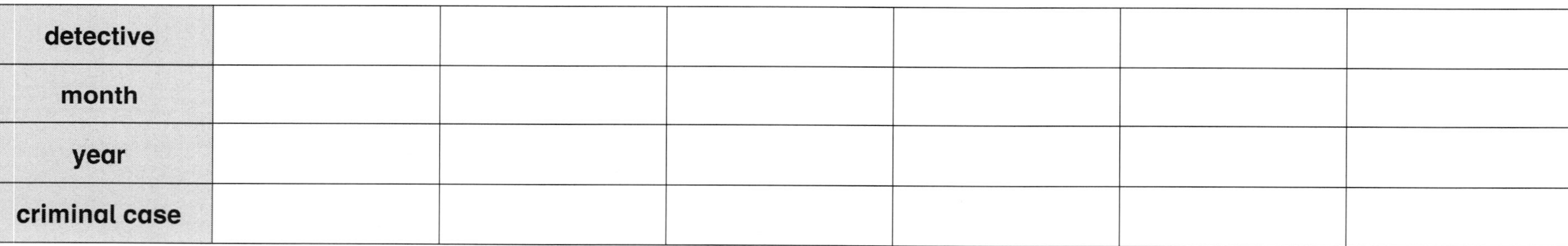

detective						
month						
year						
criminal case						

1. Between the book about the Famous Five and the book about The Three Investigators is a book about Sherlock Holmes.
2. One criminal case was solved in November 1936.
3. A book about Miss Marple is on the left.
4. The detective who solved a criminal case in December is between the ones who solved a criminal case in January and the ones who solved a criminal case in May 1999.
5. Between the blackmail and the murder is a criminal case of kidnapping.
6. Adrian Monk solved a criminal case in September 2012.
7. Between the case of 1999 and the case of 1982 is the case of 1888.
8. The criminal case of fraud is next to the criminal case of murder.
9. Next to the book about Miss Marple is a book about the Famous Five.
10. The detective who solved a criminal case in June is between the detective who solved a criminal case in September and the ones who solved a criminal case in January.
11. The blackmail was solved in 1941.
12. The book about Hercule Poirot is next to the book about The Three Investigators.
13. The criminal case of burglary is not next to the criminal case of fraud.

Lösungen

Detectives

Children are fascinated by crime stories. This child collects books about famous detectives. In each book a detective solved a criminal case in a specific month. Read, fill in the table and find out:

Who solved a robbery? **Miss Marple**
Possible solution: 2/8/5/11/4/10/7/1/9/6/3

detective	Miss Marple	Famous Five	Sherlock Holmes	The Three Investigators	Hercule Poirot	Adrian Monk
month	November	May	December	January	June	September
criminal case	**robbery**	fraud	murder	kidnapping	blackmail	burglary

2. A book about Miss Marple is on the left.
8. Next to the book about Miss Marple is a book about the Famous Five.
5. Between the book about the Famous Five and the book about The Three Investigators is a book about Sherlock Holmes.
11. The book about Hercule Poirot is next to the book about The Three Investigators.
4. Adrian Monk solved a criminal case in September.
10. Next to the detective who solved a criminal case in September is a detective who solved a criminal case in June.
7. The detectives who solved a criminal case in January are between the detective who solved a criminal case in June and the detective who solved a criminal case in December.
1. The detective who solved a criminal case in November is not next to the detective who solved a criminal case in December.
9. The fraud was solved in May.
6. The detective who solved a murder is between the detectives who solved a fraud and the detectives who solved a kidnapping.
3. The detective who solved a blackmail is between the detectives who solved a kidnapping and the detective who solved a burglary.

Detectives

Children are fascinated by crime stories. This child collects books about famous detectives. In each book a detective solved a criminal case in a specific month and year. Read, fill in the table and find out:

Who solved a robbery? **Miss Marple**
Possible solution: 3/9/1/12/6/10/4/2/7/11/5/8/13

detective	Miss Marple	Famous Five	Sherlock Holmes	The Three Investigators	Hercule Poirot	Adrian Monk
month	November	May	December	January	June	September
year	1936	1999	1888	1982	1941	2012
criminal case	**robbery**	fraud	murder	kidnapping	blackmail	burglary

3. A book about Miss Marple is on the left.
9. Next to the book about Miss Marple is a book about the Famous Five.
1. Between the book about the Famous Five and the book about The Three Investigators is a book about Sherlock Holmes.
12. The book about Hercule Poirot is next to the book about The Three Investigators.
6. Adrian Monk solved a criminal case in September 2012.
10. The detective who solved a criminal case in June is between the detective who solved a criminal case in September and the ones who solved a criminal case in January.
4. The detective who solved a criminal case in December is between the ones who solved a criminal case in January and the ones who solved a criminal case in May 1999.
2. One criminal case was solved in November 1936.
7. Between the case of 1999 and the case of 1982 is the case of 1888.
11. The blackmail was solved in 1941.
5. Between the blackmail and the murder is a criminal case of kidnapping.
8. The criminal case of fraud is next to the criminal case of murder.
13. The criminal case of burglary is not next to the criminal case of fraud.

Favourite jobs

These teenagers from different countries have nearly finished school. Now they think about what they might do for a living. There are jobs they favour and jobs they would not like to do. Read, fill in the table and find out:

Who would not like to be a librarian? ______________________

name					
country					
favourite job					
no favourite job					

1. Jessica is from England.
2. Next to the teenager who would like to be a doctor is a teenager who would like to be a teacher.
3. The teenager who would not like to be an architect is next to the one who would not like to be a zoo keeper.
4. Scarlett is on the right and next to Lucas.
5. The teenager who would like to be a hair stylist is between the one who would like to be a writer and the one who would like to be a doctor.
6. The teenager from Ireland is between the one from England and the one from Norway.
7. The teenager who would not like to be a secretary is between the one who would not like to be a cook and the one who would not like to be a zoo keeper.
8. Evie is between Lucas and Riley.
9. The teenager from Iceland would like to be a writer.
10. One teenager would like to be a nurse, but would not like to be a cook.
11. The teenager from Italy is next to the one from Norway.

Favourite jobs

These teenagers from different countries have nearly finished school. Now they think about what they might do for a living. There are jobs they favour and jobs they would not like to do. Read, fill in the table and find out:

Who would not like to be a librarian? ____________________

name						
country						
favourite job						
no favourite job						

1. The teenager from Italy is between the one from Norway and the one from Iceland.
2. Benjamin is on the right next to Scarlett.
3. Between the teenager who would like to be a football player and the one who would like to be a hair stylist is a teenager who would like to be a writer.
4. The teenager who would not like to be a secretary is between the one who would not like to be a cook and the one who would not like to be a zoo keeper.
5. Lucas is between Scarlett and Evie.
6. The teenager who would not like to be an architect is next to the one who would not like to be a zoo keeper.
7. One teenager would like to be a nurse, but would not like to be a cook.
8. Riley is next to Evie.
9. The teenager who would like to be a doctor is between the one who would like to be a hair stylist and the one who would like to be a teacher.
10. The teenager from Germany would like to be a football player.
11. Jessica is from England.
12. The teenager who would not like to be a dentist is not next to the one who would not like to be an architect.
13. The teenager from Ireland is between the one from England and the one from Norway.

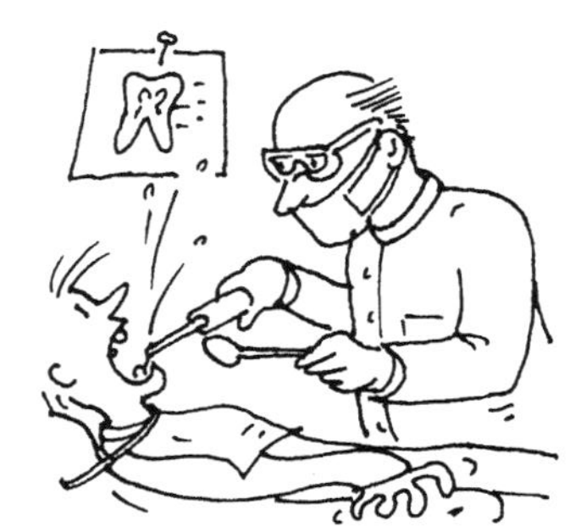

Favourite jobs

These teenagers from different countries have nearly finished school. Now they think about what they might do for a living. There are jobs they favour and jobs they would not like to do. Read, fill in the table and find out:

Who would not like to be a librarian? **Scarlett**
Possible solution: 4/8/1/6/11/9/5/2/10/7/3

name	Jessica	Riley	Evie	Lucas	**Scarlett**
country	England	Ireland	Norway	Italy	Iceland
favourite job	nurse	teacher	doctor	hair stylist	writer
no favourite job	cook	secretary	zoo keeper	architect	**librarian**

4. Scarlett is on the right and next to Lucas.
8. Evie is between Lucas and Riley.
1. Jessica is from England.
6. The teenager from Ireland is between the one from England and the one from Norway.
11. The teenager from Italy is next to the one from Norway.
9. The teenager from Iceland would like to be a writer.
5. The teenager who would like to be a hair stylist is between the one who would like to be a writer and the one who would like to be a doctor.
2. Next to the teenager who would like to be a doctor is a teenager who would like to be a teacher.
10. One teenager would like to be a nurse, but would not like to be a cook.
7. The teenager who would not like to be a secretary is between the one who would not like to be a cook and the one who would not like to be a zoo keeper.
3. The teenager who would not like to be an architect is next to the one who would not like to be a zoo keeper.

Favourite jobs

These teenagers from different countries have nearly finished school. Now they think about what they might do for a living. There are jobs they favour and jobs they would not like to do. Read, fill in the table and find out:

Who would not like to be a librarian? **Scarlett**
Possible solution: 2/5/8/11/13/1/10/3/9/7/4/6/12

name	Jessica	Riley	Evie	Lucas	**Scarlett**	Benjamin
country	England	Ireland	Norway	Italy	Iceland	Germany
favourite job	nurse	teacher	doctor	hair stylist	writer	football player
no favourite job	cook	secretary	zoo keeper	architect	**librarian**	dentist

2. Benjamin is on the right next to Scarlett.
5. Lucas is between Scarlett and Evie.
8. Riley is next to Evie.
11. Jessica is from England.
13. The teenager from Ireland is between the one from England and the one from Norway.
1. The teenager from Italy is between the one from Norway and the one from Iceland.
10. The teenager from Germany would like to be a football player.
3. Between the teenager who would like to be a football player and the one who would like to be a hair stylist is a teenager who would like to be a writer.
9. The teenager who would like to be a doctor is between the one who would like to be a hair stylist and the one who would like to be a teacher.
7. One teenager would like to be a nurse, but would not like to be a cook.
4. The teenager who would not like to be a secretary is between the one who would not like to be a cook and the one who would not like to be a zoo keeper.
6. The teenager who would not like to be an architect is next to the one who would not like to be a zoo keeper.
12. The teenager who would not like to be a dentist is not next to the one who would not like to be an architect.

Favourite teachers

There are and always will be subjects at school which children like or dislike. But as important as the subjects are the teachers. There are popular teachers at every school. Read, fill in the table and find out:

Who favours the Music teacher? ______________________

	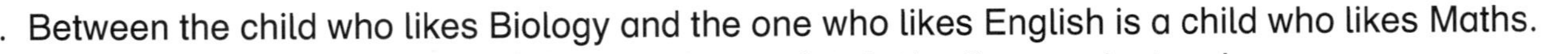				
name					
likes					
dislikes					
favourite teacher					

1. Between the child who likes Biology and the one who likes English is a child who likes Maths.
2. One child dislikes French, but her favourite teacher is the Geography teacher.
3. Next to the child who favours the Biology teacher is a child who favours the English teacher.
4. Elizabeth likes Biology.
5. The child who dislikes Spanish is between the one who dislikes Geography and the one who dislikes Art.
6. Freya is on the left and next to her is Daisy.
7. Between the child who favours the Geography teacher and the one who favours the Biology teacher is a child who favours the Spanish teacher.
8. The child who likes Physical Education is next to the one who likes English.
9. Jake is between Daisy and Sebastian.
10. The child who dislikes Chemistry is next to the one who dislikes Art.
11. One child likes German but dislikes Geography.

Favourite teachers

There are and always will be subjects at school which children like or dislike. But as important as the subjects are the teachers. There are popular teachers at every school. Read, fill in the table and find out:

Who favours the Music teacher? ______________

name						
likes						
dislikes						
favourite teacher						

1. Toby likes History.
2. Freya is on the left and next to her is Daisy.
3. The child who dislikes Chemistry is between the one who dislikes Art and the one who dislikes French.
4. Next to the child who favours the Biology teacher is a child who favours the English teacher.
5. Between the child who likes Maths and the one who likes Physical Education is a child who likes English.
6. Jake is between Daisy and Sebastian.
7. One child likes German but dislikes Geography.
8. One boy favours the Biology teacher.
9. The child who dislikes Spanish is between the one who dislikes Geography and the one who dislikes Art.
10. Elizabeth is next to Sebastian.
11. Between the child who favours the Art teacher and the one who favours the Spanish teacher is a child who favours the Geography teacher.
12. Between the child who likes History and the one who likes Maths is a child who likes Biology.
13. One child dislikes Religious Education, but his favourite teacher is the Art teacher.

Lösungen

Favourite teachers

There are and always will be subjects at school which children like or dislike. But as important as the subjects are the teachers. There are popular teachers at every school. Read, fill in the table and find out:

Who favours the Music teacher? **Freya**
Possible solution: 6/9/4/1/8/11/5/10/2/7/3

name	**Freya**	Daisy	Jake	Sebastian	Elizabeth
likes	German	Physical Education	English	Maths	Biology
dislikes	Geography	Spanish	Art	Chemistry	French
favourite teacher	**Music teacher**	English teacher	Biology teacher	Spanish teacher	Geography teacher

6. Freya is on the left and next to her is Daisy.
9. Jake is between Daisy and Sebastian.
4. Elizabeth likes Biology.
1. Between the child who likes Biology and the one who likes English is a child who likes Maths.
8. The child who likes Physical Education is next to the one who likes English.
11. One child likes German but dislikes Geography.
5. The child who dislikes Spanish is between the one who dislikes Geography and the one who dislikes Art.
10. The child who dislikes Chemistry is next to the one who dislikes Art.
2. One child dislikes French, but her favourite teacher is the Geography teacher.
7. Between the child who favours the Geography teacher and the one who favours the Biology teacher is a child who favours the Spanish teacher.
3. Next to the child who favours the Biology teacher is a child who favours the English teacher.

Favourite teachers

There are and always will be subjects at school which children like or dislike. But as important as the subjects are the teachers. There are popular teachers at every school. Read, fill in the table and find out:

Who favours the Music teacher? **Freya**
Possible solution: 2/6/10/1/12/5/7/9/3/13/11/8/4

name	**Freya**	Daisy	Jake	Sebastian	Elizabeth	Toby
likes	German	Physical Education	English	Maths	Biology	History
dislikes	Geography	Spanish	Art	Chemistry	French	Religious Education
favourite teacher	**Music teacher**	English teacher	Biology teacher	Spanish teacher	Geography teacher	Art teacher

2. Freya is on the left and next to her is Daisy.
6. Jake is between Daisy and Sebastian.
10. Elizabeth is next to Sebastian.
1. Toby likes History.
12. Between the child who likes History and the one who likes Maths is a child who likes Biology.
5. Between the child who likes Maths and the one who likes Physical Education is a child who likes English.
7. One child likes German but dislikes Geography.
9. The child who dislikes Spanish is between the one who dislikes Geography and the one who dislikes Art.
3. The child who dislikes Chemistry is between the one who dislikes Art and the one who dislikes French.
13. One child dislikes Religious Education, but his favourite teacher is the Art teacher.
11. Between the child who favours the Art teacher and the one who favours the Spanish teacher is a child who favours the Geography teacher.
8. One boy favours the Biology teacher.
4. Next to the child who favours the Biology teacher is a child who favours the English teacher.

Flowers

In these vases you can see different flowers. Flowers can make your life more beautiful.
Colour the leaves and shafts green.
Read the hints, colour the flowers and vases and find out:

In which vase are purple pinks and a yellow lily? ______________________

1. Red gerberas are between yellow gerberas and orange gerberas.
2. The blue vase is between the brown vase and the black vase.
3. Yellow roses and blue tulips are between the vase with the yellow tulips and the vase with the orange tulips and white roses.
4. Next to the orange lily are red pinks.
5. The vase on the right is brown.
6. The orange pinks are not next to the red pinks.
7. Pink roses, white tulips and yellow gerberas are in the same vase.
8. The blue lily is in the vase with the orange pinks.
9. In the white vase are red roses and yellow tulips.
10. The white lily is not next to the blue lily.
11. White gerberas, green pinks and an orange lily are in the same vase.

Flowers

In these vases you can see different flowers. Flowers can make your life more beautiful.
Colour the leaves and shafts green.
Read the hints, colour the flowers and vases and find out:

In which vase are purple pinks and a yellow lily? ______________________

1. Next to the orange gerberas is a vase with pink gerberas and yellow pinks.
2. Orange pinks and a blue lily are not next to the white lily.
3. The blue vase is between the brown vase and the black vase.
4. Orange roses and purple tulips are between the vase with the yellow tulips and the vase with the blue tulips and yellow roses.
5. In the white vase are red roses and yellow tulips.
6. The vase on the right is brown.
7. Pink roses, white tulips and yellow gerberas are in the same vase.
8. Next to the orange lily is a red lily.
9. Next to the yellow roses is a vase with white roses and orange tulips.
10. The grey vase is next to the black vase.
11. White gerberas, green pinks and an orange lily are in the same vase.
12. Red gerberas are between yellow gerberas and orange gerberas.
13. Red pinks and a white lily are in the vase next to the red lily.

Flowers

In these vases you can see different flowers. Flowers can make your life more beautiful.
Colour the leaves and shafts green.
Read the hints, colour the flowers and vases and find out:

In which vase are purple pinks and a yellow lily? **In the blue vase**
Possible solution: 5/2/9/3/7/1/11/4/6/8/10

vase	white	black	**blue**	brown
roses	red	yellow	white	pink
tulips	yellow	blue	orange	white
gerberas	white	orange	red	yellow
pinks	green	red	**purple**	orange
lily	orange	white	**yellow**	blue

5. The vase on the right is brown.
2. The blue vase is between the brown vase and the black vase.
9. In the white vase are red roses and yellow tulips.
3. Yellow roses and blue tulips are between the vase with the yellow tulips and the vase with the orange tulips and white roses.
7. Pink roses, white tulips and yellow gerberas are in the same vase.
1. Red gerberas are between yellow gerberas and orange gerberas.
11. White gerberas, green pinks and an orange lily are in the same vase.
4. Next to the orange lily are red pinks.
6. The orange pinks are not next to the red pinks.
8. The blue lily is in the vase with the orange pinks.
10. The white lily is not next to the blue lily.

Flowers

In these vases you can see different flowers. Flowers can make your life more beautiful.
Colour the leaves and shafts green.
Read the hints, colour the flowers and vases and find out:

In which vase are purple pinks and a yellow lily? **In the blue vase**
Possible solution: 6/3/10/5/4/9/7/12/1/11/8/13/2

vase	white	grey	black	**blue**	brown
roses	red	orange	yellow	white	pink
tulips	yellow	purple	blue	orange	white
gerberas	white	pink	orange	red	yellow
pinks	green	yellow	red	**purple**	orange
lily	orange	red	white	**yellow**	blue

6. The vase on the right is brown.
3. The blue vase is between the brown vase and the black vase.
10. The grey vase is next to the black vase.
5. In the white vase are red roses and yellow tulips.
4. Orange roses and purple tulips are between the vase with the yellow tulips and the vase with the blue tulips and yellow roses.
9. Next to the yellow roses is a vase with white roses and orange tulips.
7. Pink roses, white tulips and yellow gerberas are in the same vase.
12. Red gerberas are between yellow gerberas and orange gerberas.
1. Next to the orange gerberas is a vase with pink gerberas and yellow pinks.
11. White gerberas, green pinks and an orange lily are in the same vase.
8. Next to the orange lily is a red lily.
13. Red pinks and a white lily are in the vase next to the red lily.
2. Orange pinks and a blue lily are not next to the white lily.

Football kits

Boys and girls like football. Very popular are the football kits that make your outfit special.
Look at these boys and girls, colour their footballs, football kits (T-shirt and shorts), socks and trainers and find out:

Who has a yellow football kit? ____________

name: ____________ **name:** ____________ **name:** ____________ **name:** ____________

1. One child has a green football and brown football socks.
2. Between the child with black trainers and the child with brown trainers is a child with blue trainers.
3. Daniel is on the right and next to him is Phoebe.
4. The child with a red football is between the child with a blue football and the one with a yellow football.
5. The child with a red football kit is not next to the child with an orange football kit.
6. Oliver has a blue football.
7. Noah is next to Phoebe.
8. One child has yellow football socks and black trainers.
9. The child with an orange football kit is next to the child with a blue football kit.
10. One child has yellow trainers and a blue football kit.
11. The child with blue football socks is between the one with brown football socks and the one with green football socks.

Football kits

Boys and girls like football. Very popular are the football kits that make your outfit special.
Look at these boys and girls, colour their footballs, football kits (T-shirt and shorts), socks and trainers and find out:

Who has a yellow football kit? ____________

name: ________ name: ________ name: ________ name: ________ name: ________

1. The child with brown football socks is between the one with black football socks and the one with blue football socks.
2. Between the child with black trainers and the child with brown trainers is a child with blue trainers.
3. Holly is on the right and next to her is Daniel.
4. The child with a red football is between the child with a blue football and the one with a yellow football.
5. Next to the child with blue football socks is a child with green football socks.
6. The child with a red football kit is not next to the child with an orange football kit.
7. The child with yellow trainers is between the child with brown trainers and the child that has purple trainers and a green football kit.
8. Phoebe is between Daniel and Noah.
9. The child with an orange football has black football socks.
10. One child has yellow football socks and black trainers.
11. Oliver has a blue football.
12. The child with a blue football kit is between the child with a green football kit and the one with an orange football kit.
13. The child with a green football is next to the one with a yellow football.

Lösungen

Football kits

Boys and girls like football. Very popular are the football kits that make your outfit special.
Look at these boys and girls, colour their footballs, football kits (T-shirt and shorts), socks and trainers and find out:

Who has a yellow football kit? **Noah**
Possible solution: 3/7/6/4/1/11/8/2/10/9/5

name	Oliver	**Noah**	Phoebe	Daniel
football	blue	red	yellow	green
football socks	yellow	green	blue	brown
trainers	black	blue	brown	yellow
football kit	red	**yellow**	orange	blue

3. Daniel is on the right and next to him is Phoebe.
7. Noah is next to Phoebe.
6. Oliver has a blue football.
4. The child with a red football is between the child with a blue football and the one with a yellow football.
1. One child has a green football and brown football socks.
11. The child with blue football socks is between the one with brown football socks and the one with green football socks.
8. One child has yellow football socks and black trainers.
2. Between the child with black trainers and the child with brown trainers is a child with blue trainers.
10. One child has yellow trainers and a blue football kit.
9. The child with an orange football kit is next to the child with a blue football kit.
5. The child with a red football kit is not next to the child with an orange football kit.

Football kits

Boys and girls like football. Very popular are the football kits that make your outfit special.
Look at these boys and girls, colour their footballs, football kits (T-shirt and shorts), socks and trainers and find out:

Who has a yellow football kit? **Noah**
Possible solution: 3/8/11/4/13/9/1/5/10/2/7/12/6

name	Oliver	**Noah**	Phoebe	Daniel	Holly
football	blue	red	yellow	green	orange
football socks	yellow	green	blue	brown	black
trainers	black	blue	brown	yellow	purple
football kit	red	**yellow**	orange	blue	green

3. Holly is on the right and next to her is Daniel.
8. Phoebe is between Daniel and Noah.
11. Oliver has a blue football.
4. The child with a red football is between the child with a blue football and the one with a yellow football.
13. The child with a green football is next to the one with a yellow football.
9. The child with an orange football has black football socks.
1. The child with brown football socks is between the one with black football socks and the one with blue football socks.
5. Next to the child with blue football socks is a child with green football socks.
10. One child has yellow football socks and black trainers.
2. Between the child with black trainers and the child with brown trainers is a child with blue trainers.
7. The child with yellow trainers is between the child with brown trainers and the child that has purple trainers and a green football kit.
12. The child with a blue football kit is between the child with a green football kit and the one with an orange football kit.
6. The child with a red football kit is not next to the child with an orange football kit.

Hobbies

Children in year seven at the new school get to know each other better in the first few months of the term. They talk about their birthdays and various hobbies. Each of them has two hobbies.
Read, fill in the table and find out:

Whose hobby is riding a horse? ______________________

name					
birthday month					
hobby 1					
hobby 2					

1. The child whose birthday is in June is between the child whose birthday is in January and the one whose birthday is in May.
2. The child who likes listening to CDs is next to the child who likes taking photos.
3. The child who likes playing online games is between the child who likes playing video games and the one who likes chatting on Facebook.
4. One child has his birthday in April and likes making music and reading books.
5. The boy on the left is James.
6. Joseph's birthday is in January.
7. The child whose birthday is in December is next to the child whose birthday is in May.
8. One child likes collecting autographs and playing video games.
9. Between James and Megan is Hannah.
10. The child who likes meeting friends is between the one who likes making music and the one who likes taking photos.
11. Oliver is next to Megan.

Hobbies

Children in year seven at the new school get to know each other better in the first few months of the term. They talk about their birthdays and various hobbies. Each of them has two hobbies. Read, fill in the table and find out:

Whose hobby is riding a horse? ____________

name						
birthday month						
hobby 1						
hobby 2						

1. Joseph's birthday is in January.
2. The girl on the left is Lucy.
3. The child who likes making music is between the child who likes painting and the one who likes meeting friends.
4. Between the child whose birthday is in May and the one whose birthday is in April is a child whose birthday is in December.
5. One boy likes reading books.
6. Between Lucy and Hannah is James.
7. One child has her birthday in February and likes painting.
8. The child who likes playing online games is between the child who likes playing video games and the one who likes chatting on Facebook.
9. Between the child who likes meeting friends and the one who likes listening to CDs is a child who likes taking photos.
10. Megan is between Hannah and Oliver.
11. The child who likes playing the guitar is on the left next to the child who likes reading books.
12. One child likes collecting autographs and playing video games.
13. The child whose birthday is in June is between the child whose birthday is in January and the child whose birthday is in May.

Hobbies

Children in year seven at the new school get to know each other better in the first few months of the term. They talk about their birthdays and various hobbies. Each of them has two hobbies. Read, fill in the table and find out:

Whose hobby is riding a horse? **It's Hannah's hobby**
Possible solution: 5/9/11/6/1/7/4/10/2/8/3

name	James	**Hannah**	Megan	Oliver	Joseph
birthday month	April	December	May	June	January
hobby 1	making music	meeting friends	taking photos	listening to CDs	collecting autographs
hobby 2	reading books	**riding a horse**	chatting on Facebook	playing online games	playing video games

5. The boy on the left is James.
9. Between James and Megan is Hannah.
11. Oliver is next to Megan.
6. Joseph's birthday is in January.
1. The child whose birthday is in June is between the child whose birthday is in January and the one whose birthday is in May.
7. The child whose birthday is in December is next to the child whose birthday is in May.
4. One child has his birthday in April and likes making music and reading books.
10. The child who likes meeting friends is between the one who likes making music and the one who likes taking photos.
2. The child who likes listening to CDs is next to the child who likes taking photos.
8. One child likes collecting autographs and playing video games.
3. The child who likes playing online games is between the child who likes playing video games and the one who likes chatting on Facebook.

Hobbies

Children in year seven at the new school get to know each other better in the first few months of the term. They talk about their birthdays and various hobbies. Each of them has two hobbies. Read, fill in the table and find out:

Whose hobby is riding a horse? **It's Hannah's hobby**
Possible solution: 2/6/10/1/13/4/7/3/9/12/8/5/11

name	Lucy	James	**Hannah**	Megan	Oliver	Joseph
birthday month	February	April	December	May	June	January
hobby 1	painting	making music	meeting friends	taking photos	listening to CDs	collecting auto-graphs
hobby 2	playing the guitar	reading books	**riding a horse**	chatting on Facebook	playing online games	playing video games

2. The girl on the left is Lucy.
6. Between Lucy and Hannah is James.
10. Megan is between Hannah and Oliver.
1. Joseph's birthday is in January.
13. The child whose birthday is in June is between the child whose birthday is in January and the child whose birthday is in May.
4. Between the child whose birthday is in May and the one whose birthday is in April is a child whose birthday is in December.
7. One child has her birthday in February and likes painting.
3. The child who likes making music is between the child who likes painting and the one who likes meeting friends.
9. Between the child who likes meeting friends and the one who likes listening to CDs is a child who likes taking photos.
12. One child likes collecting autographs and playing video games.
8. The child who likes playing online games is between the child who likes playing video games and the one who likes chatting on Facebook.
5. One boy likes reading books.
11. The child who likes playing the guitar is on the left next to the child who likes reading books.

Jobs at home

These children help their families by doing some jobs at home which are necessary for a nice living. But some of the jobs they don't really like doing.
Read, fill in the table and find out:

Who doesn't like taking out the rubbish? ____________________

name					
day of the week					
job they like					
job they don't like					

1. The child that likes making the beds is between the child that likes walking the dog and the one that likes making breakfast.
2. Dylan is on the right and helps at home on Saturdays.
3. Ava helps at home on Fridays and is next to the child who helps on Mondays.
4. One child likes going shopping, but doesn't like doing the washing.
5. Tyler is between Dylan and Ruby.
6. One child helps on Wednesdays and likes walking the dog.
7. The child that doesn't like laying the table is between the one that doesn't like doing the washing and the one that doesn't like cooking.
8. Adam is next to Ruby.
9. One boy doesn't like washing the dishes.
10. Next to the child that likes making breakfast is a child that likes ironing.
11. The child that helps on Thursdays is next to the child that helps on Mondays.

Jobs at home

These children help their families by doing some jobs at home which are necessary for a nice living. But some of the jobs they don't really like doing.
Read, fill in the table and find out:

Who doesn't like taking out the rubbish? ______________________

name						
day of the week						
job they like						
job they don't like						

1. Arthur helps at home on Tuesdays and is next to the child who helps on Fridays.
2. Next to the child that doesn't like cooking is a child that doesn't like washing the dishes.
3. The child that likes ironing is next to the child that likes making breakfast.
4. Dylan is on the right and helps at home on Saturdays.
5. Adam is between Ruby and Ava.
6. The child that doesn't like laying the table is between the child that doesn't like doing the washing and the one that doesn't like cooking.
7. The child that doesn't like watering the plants is not next to the child that doesn't like washing the dishes.
8. The child that likes making the beds is between the child that likes walking the dog and the one that likes making breakfast.
9. The child that helps on Mondays is between the one who helps on Fridays and the one who helps on Thursdays.
10. Tyler is between Dylan and Ruby.
11. One child likes going shopping but doesn't like doing the washing.
12. The child that helps on Wednesdays likes walking the dog.
13. Next to the child that likes ironing is a child that likes vacuum cleaning the flat.

Lösungen

Jobs at home

These children help their families by doing some jobs at home which are necessary for a nice living. But some of the jobs they don't really like doing.
Read, fill in the table and find out:

Who doesn't like taking out the rubbish? **Ava**
Possible solution: 2/5/8/3/11/6/1/10/4/7/9

name	**Ava**	Adam	Ruby	Tyler	Dylan
day of the week	Fridays	Mondays	Thursdays	Wednesdays	Saturdays
job they like	ironing	making breakfast	making the beds	walking the dog	going shopping
job they don't like	**taking out the rubbish**	washing the dishes	cooking	laying the table	doing the washing

2. Dylan is on the right and helps at home on Saturdays.
5. Tyler is between Dylan and Ruby.
8. Adam is next to Ruby.
3. Ava helps at home on Fridays and is next to the child who helps on Mondays.
11. The child that helps on Thursdays is next to the child that helps on Mondays.
6. One child helps on Wednesdays and likes walking the dog.
1. The child that likes making the beds is between the child that likes walking the dog and the one that likes making breakfast.
10. Next to the child that likes making breakfast is a child that likes ironing.
4. One child likes going shopping, but doesn't like doing the washing.
7. The child that doesn't like laying the table is between the one that doesn't like doing the washing and the one that doesn't like cooking.
9. One boy doesn't like washing the dishes.

Jobs at home

These children help their families by doing some jobs at home which are necessary for a nice living. But some of the jobs they don't really like doing.
Read, fill in the table and find out:

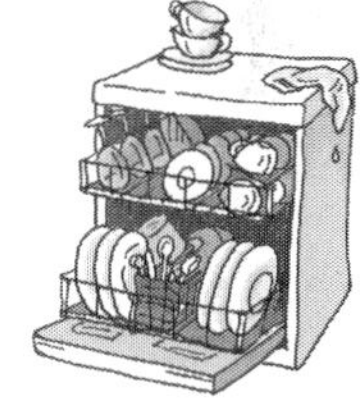

Who doesn't like taking out the rubbish? **Ava**
Possible solution: 4/10/5/1/9/12/8/3/13/11/6/2/7

name	Arthur	**Ava**	Adam	Ruby	Tyler	Dylan
day of the week	Tuesdays	Fridays	Mondays	Thursdays	Wednesdays	Saturdays
job they like	vacuum cleaning the flat	ironing	making breakfast	making the beds	walking the dog	going shopping
job they don't like	watering the plants	**taking out the rubbish**	washing the dishes	cooking	laying the table	doing the washing

4. Dylan is on the right and helps at home on Saturdays.
10. Tyler is between Dylan and Ruby.
5. Adam is between Ruby and Ava.
1. Arthur helps at home on Tuesdays and is next to the child who helps on Fridays.
9. The child that helps on Mondays is between the one who helps on Fridays and the one who helps on Thursdays.
12. The child that helps on Wednesdays likes walking the dog.
8. The child that likes making the beds is between the child that likes walking the dog and the one that likes making breakfast.
3. The child that likes ironing is next to the child that likes making breakfast.
13. Next to the child that likes ironing is a child that likes vacuum cleaning the flat.
11. One child likes going shopping but doesn't like doing the washing.
6. The child that doesn't like laying the table is between the child that doesn't like doing the washing and the one that doesn't like cooking.
2. Next to the child that doesn't like cooking is a child that doesn't like washing the dishes.
7. The child that doesn't like watering the plants is not next to the child that doesn't like washing the dishes.

Laying the table

In a restaurant the tables must be prepared for the guests. You can now help the waiter laying the tables. First draw four plates on each table. Then add spoons, knives, forks, glasses and paper napkins in different amounts on each table. Read the sentences, draw and find out:

On which table are five paper napkins? ______________________

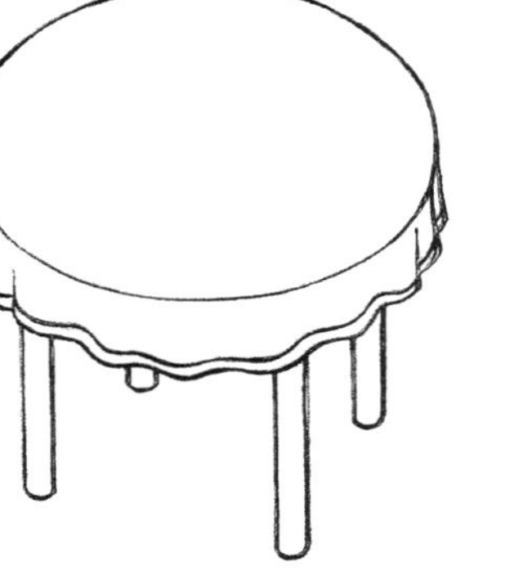
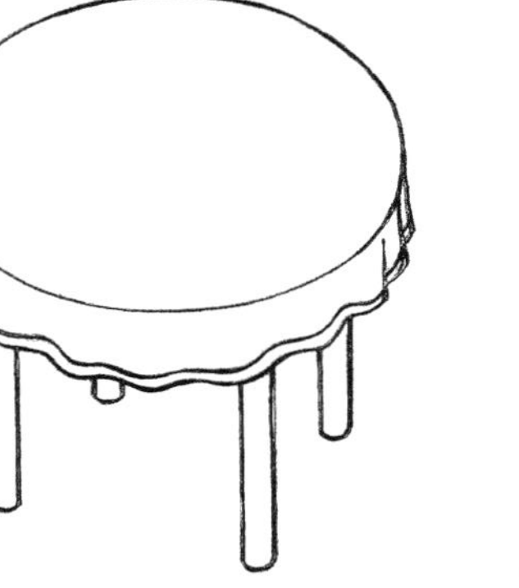
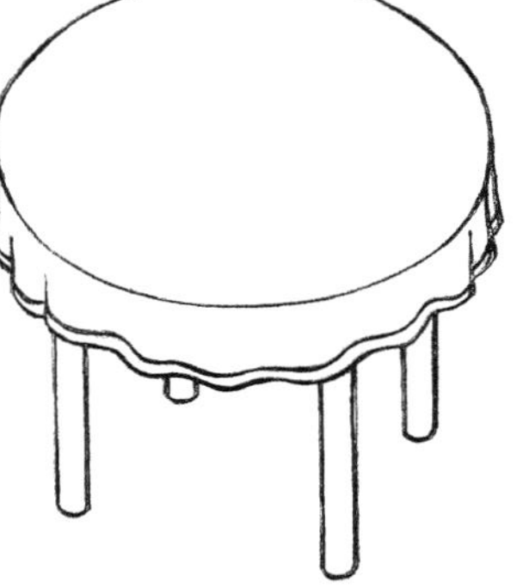
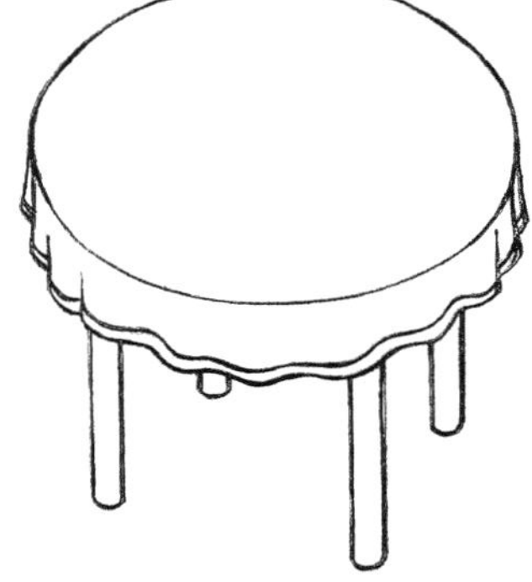
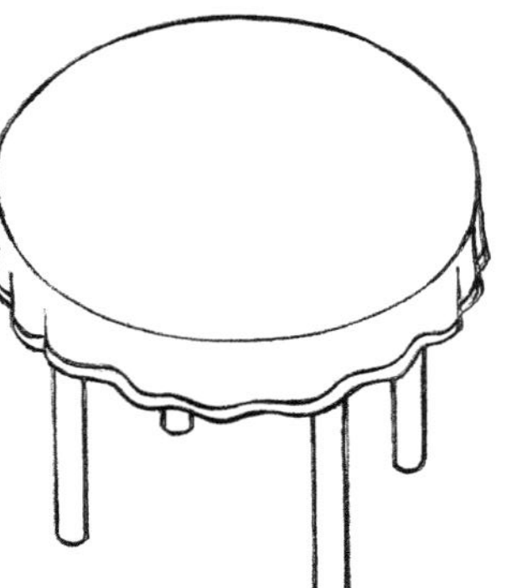
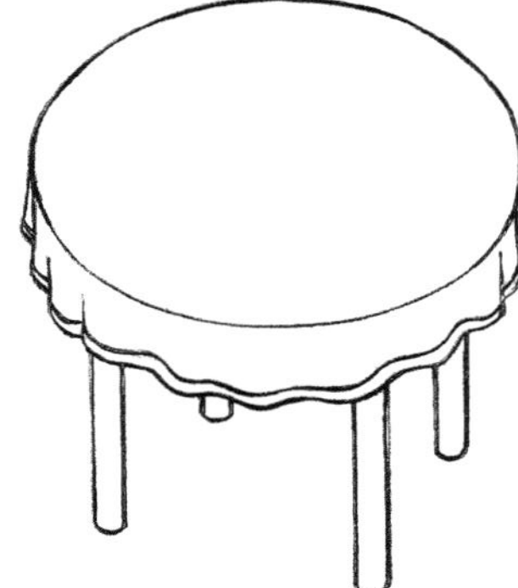
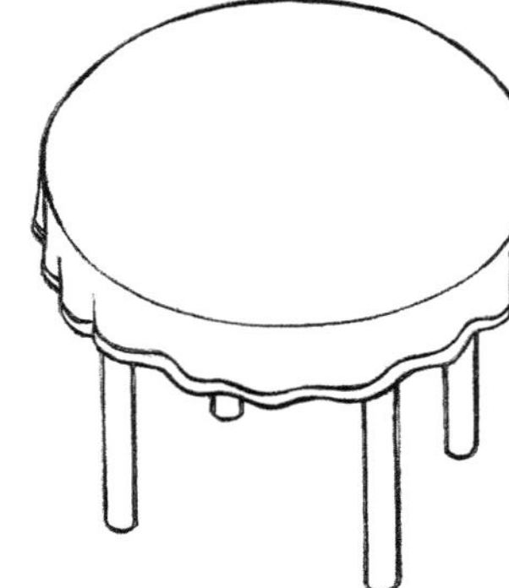
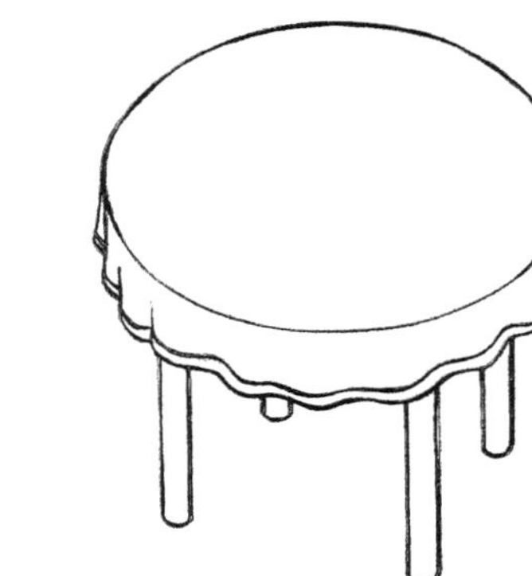

1. On the first table are four knives.
2. Between the table with four spoons and the table with five spoons is a table with two spoons.
3. Three spoons and four glasses are on the same table.
4. Between the table with four knives and the table with three knives is a table with five knives.
5. Three forks and four spoons are on the same table.
6. One glass and four paper napkins are on the same table.
7. Between the table with five forks and the table with four forks is a table with two forks.
8. Two knives and five forks are on the same table.
9. Between the table with four glasses and the table with three glasses is a table with two glasses.
10. The table with one paper napkin is not next to the table with four paper napkins.
11. The table with three paper napkins is on the right next to the table with one paper napkin.

Laying the table

In a restaurant the tables must be prepared for the guests. You can now help the waiter laying the tables.
On each table are plates, spoons, knives, forks, glasses and paper napkins in different amounts.
Read the sentences, draw and find out:

On which table are five paper napkins? ______________________

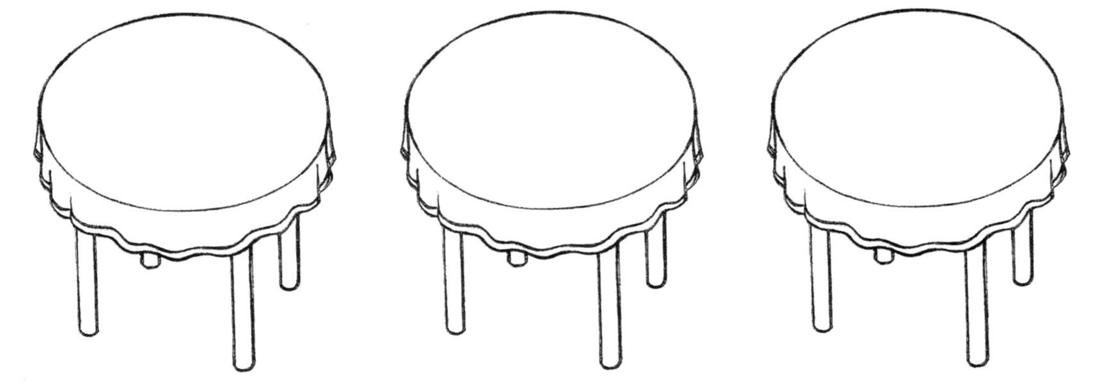

1. Four knives and three forks are on the same table.
2. On the first table are five plates.
3. Between the table with one glass and the table with two glasses is a table with three glasses.
4. Five forks and three spoons are on the same table.
5. Between the table with five plates and the table with four plates is a table with three plates.
6. The table with one paper napkin is next to the table with three paper napkins.
7. Between the table with three forks and the table with two forks is a table with four forks.
8. Four spoons and one glass are on the same table.
9. One plate and two knives are on the same table.
10. Between the table with three spoons and the table with two spoons is a table with five spoons.
11. Between the table with two knives and the table with five knives is a table with three knives.
12. The table with four paper napkins is not next to the table with one paper napkin.
13. Four glasses and three paper napkins are on the same table.

Laying the table

In a restaurant the tables must be prepared for the guests. You can now help the waiter laying the tables. First draw four plates on each table. Then add spoons, knives, forks, glasses and paper napkins in different amounts on each table.
Read the sentences, draw and find out:

On which table are five paper napkins? **On table 2**
Possible solution: 1/4/8/7/5/2/3/9/6/10/11

	table 1	table 2	table 3	table 4
knives	4	5	3	2
forks	3	4	2	5
spoons	4	2	5	3
glasses	1	3	2	4
paper napkins	4	**5**	1	3

1. On the first table are four knives.
4. Between the table with four knives and the table with three knives is a table with five knives.
8. Two knives and five forks are on the same table.
7. Between the table with five forks and the table with four forks is a table with two forks.
5. Three forks and four spoons are on the same table.
2. Between the table with four spoons and the table with five spoons is a table with two spoons.
3. Three spoons and four glasses are on the same table.
9. Between the table with four glasses and the table with three glasses is a table with two glasses.
6. One glass and four paper napkins are on the same table.
10. The table with one paper napkin is not next to the table with four paper napkins.
11. The table with three paper napkins is on the right next to the table with one paper napkin.

Laying the table

In a restaurant the tables must be prepared for the guests. You can now help the waiter laying the tables. On each table are plates, spoons, knives, forks, glasses and paper napkins in different amounts.
Read the sentences, draw and find out:

On which table are five paper napkins? **On table 2**
Possible solution: 2/5/9/11/1/7/4/10/8/3/13/6/12

	table 1	table 2	table 3	table 4
plates	5	3	4	1
knives	4	5	3	2
forks	3	4	2	5
spoons	4	2	5	3
glasses	1	3	2	4
paper napkins	4	**5**	1	3

2. On the first table are five plates.
5. Between the table with five plates and the table with four plates is a table with three plates.
9. One plate and two knives are on the same table.
11. Between the table with two knives and the table with five knives is a table with three knives.
1. Four knives and three forks are on the same table.
7. Between the table with three forks and the table with two forks is a table with four forks.
4. Five forks and three spoons are on the same table.
10. Between the table with three spoons and the table with two spoons is a table with five spoons.
8. Four spoons and one glass are on the same table.
3. Between the table with one glass and the table with two glasses is a table with three glasses.
13. Four glasses and three paper napkins are on the same table.
6. The table with one paper napkin is next to the table with three paper napkins.
12. The table with four paper napkins is not next to the table with one paper napkin.

London

Visiting London and all of its sights is a dream of a lot of people. These teenagers make their dream come true and go to London for one day. They visit different sights on different days and take various means of transports to get there. Read, fill in the table and find out:

Who visits the Houses of Parliament? ____________________

name					
day					
transport					
sight					

1. Matilda is next to Freddie.
2. The child who visits London on a Saturday is between the one who visits London on a Wednesday and the one who visits London on a Monday.
3. The child who visits London on a Tuesday takes the boat to Greenwich.
4. Eva is the girl on the left and next to Florence.
5. The child who goes on foot is next to the one who takes the bus.
6. The child who takes the tube is between the one who takes the boat and the one who takes the bus.
7. The child who visits Speaker's Corner is between the one who visits the Tower of London and the one who visits Piccadilly Circus.
8. Next to the child who visits London on a Monday is a child who visits London on a Thursday.
9. Florence is next to Freddie.
10. One child takes the taxi and visits the Tower of London.
11. Isaac visits London on a Wednesday.

London

Visiting London and all of its sights is a dream of a lot of people. These teenagers make their dream come true and go to London for one day. They visit different sights on different days and take various means of transports to get there. Read, fill in the table and find out:

Who visits the Houses of Parliament? ______________

name						
day						
transport						
sight						

1. Max visits London on a Friday.
2. Between the child who visits London on a Saturday and the child who visits London on a Thursday is a child who visits London on a Monday.
3. The child who goes on foot is between the one who takes the bus and the one who takes a taxi.
4. The child who visits Piccadilly Circus is next to the one that visits Speaker's Corner.
5. Florence is between Eva and Freddie.
6. Eva is the girl on the left.
7. The child who visits the Tower of London is between the one who visits London Eye and the one who visits Speaker's Corner.
8. Matilda is between Freddie and Isaac.
9. The child who visits London on a Tuesday takes the boat.
10. The child who takes the tube is between the one who takes the boat and the one who takes the bus.
11. The child who visits Greenwich is not next to the one that visits Piccadilly Circus.
12. The child who visits London on a Wednesday is between the one who visits London on a Friday and the one who visits London on Saturday.
13. One child takes the bike and visits London Eye.

Lösungen

London

Visiting London and all of its sights is a dream of a lot of people. These teenagers make their dream come true and go to London for one day. They visit different sights on different days and take various means of transports to get there. Read, fill in the table and find out:

Who visits the Houses of Parliament? **Florence**
Possible solution: 4/9/1/11/2/8/3/6/5/10/7

name	Eva	**Florence**	Freddie	Matilda	Isaac
day	Tuesday	Thursday	Monday	Saturday	Wednesday
transport	boat	tube	bus	on foot	taxi
sight	Greenwich	**Houses of Parliament**	Piccadilly Circus	Speaker's Corner	Tower of London

4. Eva is the girl on the left and next to Florence.
9. Florence is next to Freddie.
1. Matilda is next to Freddie.
11. Isaac visits London on a Wednesday.
2. The child who visits London on a Saturday is between the one who visits London on a Wednesday and the one who visits London on a Monday.
8. Next to the child who visits London on a Monday is a child who visits London on a Thursday.
3. The child who visits London on a Tuesday takes the boat to Greenwich.
6. The child who takes the tube is between the one who takes the boat and the one who takes the bus.
5. The child who goes on foot is next to the one who takes the bus.
10. One child takes the taxi and visits the Tower of London.
7. The child who visits Speaker's Corner is between the one who visits the Tower of London and the one who visits Piccadilly Circus.

London

Visiting London and all of its sights is a dream of a lot of people. These teenagers make their dream come true and go to London for one day. They visit different sights on different days and take various means of transports to get there. Read, fill in the table and find out:

Who visits the Houses of Parliament? **Florence**
Possible solution: 6/5/8/1/12/2/9/10/3/13/7/4/11

name	Eva	**Florence**	Freddie	Matilda	Isaac	Max
day	Tuesday	Thursday	Monday	Saturday	Wednesday	Friday
transport	boat	tube	bus	on foot	taxi	bike
sight	Greenwich	**Houses of Parliament**	Piccadilly Circus	Speaker's Corner	Tower of London	London Eye

6. Eva is the girl on the left.
5. Florence is between Eva and Freddie.
8. Matilda is between Freddie and Isaac.
1. Max visits London on a Friday.
12. The child who visits London on a Wednesday is between the one who visits London on a Friday and the one who visits London on Saturday.
2. Between the child who visits London on a Saturday and the child who visits London on a Thursday is a child who visits London on a Monday.
9. The child who visits London on a Tuesday takes the boat.
10. The child who takes the tube is between the one who takes the boat and the one who takes the bus.
3. The child who goes on foot is between the one who takes the bus and the one who takes a taxi.
13. One child takes the bike and visits London Eye.
7. The child who visits the Tower of London is between the one who visits London Eye and the one who visits Speaker's Corner.
4. The child who visits Piccadilly Circus is next to the one that visits Speaker's Corner.
11. The child who visits Greenwich is not next to the one that visits Piccadilly Circus.

Paintings

There are famous paintings by only using geometric shapes. Be a painter now!
In each painting there is a circle, a triangle, a rectangle and a square.
Read, draw, colour and find out:

In which painting is a red square? ______________________

painting 1 | painting 2 | painting 3 | painting 4

1. A purple rectangle and a yellow square are in the same painting.
2. The painting with the orange square is not next to the painting with the green square.
3. In the painting on the right is a blue circle.
4. A red circle and a pink triangle are in the same painting.
5. Next to the painting with the blue circle is a painting with a green circle.
6. Next to the painting with the pink rectangle is a painting with a blue rectangle.
7. Between the pink triangle and the orange triangle is a blue triangle.
8. The painting with the orange circle is next to the painting with the green circle.
9. The painting with the yellow rectangle is next to the painting with the blue rectangle.
10. Next to the painting with the yellow square is a painting with a green square.
11. A yellow triangle and a pink rectangle are in the same painting.

Paintings

There are famous paintings by only using geometric shapes. Be a painter now!
In each painting there is a circle, a triangle, a rectangle and a square.
Read, draw, colour and find out:

In which painting is a red square? ____________________

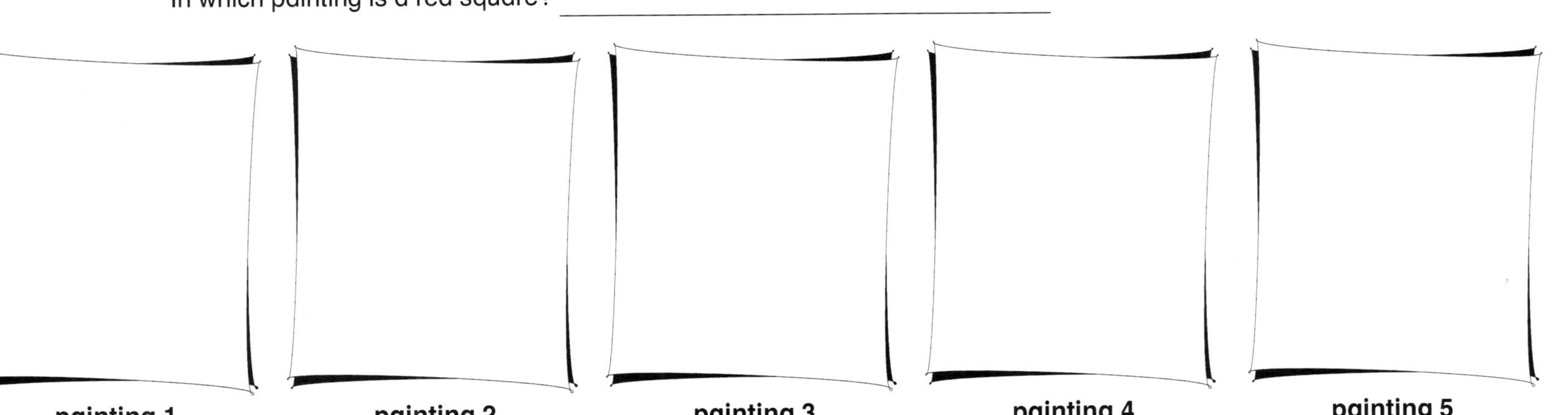

painting 1 | painting 2 | painting 3 | painting 4 | painting 5

1. Next to the painting with the blue rectangle is a painting with a yellow rectangle.
2. Next to the painting with the green circle is a painting with an orange circle.
3. The painting with the orange square is not next to the painting with the green square.
4. In the painting on the right is a yellow circle.
5. The painting with the blue square is on the right next to the painting with the orange square.
6. Between the yellow circle and the green circle is a painting with a blue circle.
7. Between the green rectangle and the blue rectangle is a painting with a pink rectangle.
8. Next to the painting with the yellow square is a painting with a green square.
9. Next to the painting with the orange triangle is a painting with a yellow triangle.
10. A red circle and a pink triangle are in the same painting.
11. A purple rectangle and a yellow square are in the same painting.
12. Between the pink triangle and the orange triangle is a blue triangle.
13. A purple triangle and a green rectangle are in the same painting.

Paintings

There are famous paintings by only using geometric shapes. Be a painter now!
In each painting there is a circle, a triangle, a rectangle and a square.
Read, draw, colour and find out:

In which painting is a red square? **In painting 3**
Possible solution: 3/5/8/4/7/11/6/9/1/10/2

	painting 1	painting 2	painting 3	painting 4
circle	red	orange	green	blue
triangle	pink	blue	orange	yellow
rectangle	purple	yellow	blue	pink
square	yellow	green	**red**	orange

3. In the painting on the right is a blue circle.
5. Next to the painting with the blue circle is a painting with a green circle.
8. The painting with the orange circle is next to the painting with the green circle.
4. A red circle and a pink triangle are in the same painting.
7. Between the pink triangle and the orange triangle is a blue triangle.
11. A yellow triangle and a pink rectangle are in the same painting.
6. Next to the painting with the pink rectangle is a painting with a blue rectangle.
9. The painting with the yellow rectangle is next to the painting with the blue rectangle.
1. A purple rectangle and a yellow square are in the same painting.
10. Next to the painting with the yellow square is a painting with a green square.
2. The painting with the orange square is not next to the painting with the green square.

Paintings

There are famous paintings by only using geometric shapes. Be a painter now!
In each painting there is a circle, a triangle, a rectangle and a square.
Read, draw, colour and find out:

In which painting is a red square? **Painting 3**
Possible solution: 4/6/2/10/12/9/13/7/1/11/8/3/5

	painting 1	painting 2	painting 3	painting 4	painting 5
circle	red	orange	green	blue	yellow
triangle	pink	blue	orange	yellow	purple
rectangle	purple	yellow	blue	pink	green
square	yellow	green	**red**	orange	blue

4. In the painting on the right is a yellow circle.
6. Between the yellow circle and the green circle is a painting with a blue circle.
2. Next to the painting with the green circle is a painting with an orange circle.
10. A red circle and a pink triangle are in the same painting.
12. Between the pink triangle and the orange triangle is a blue triangle.
9. Next to the painting with the orange triangle is a painting with a yellow triangle.
13. A purple triangle and a green rectangle are in the same painting.
7. Between the green rectangle and the blue rectangle is a painting with a pink rectangle.
1. Next to the painting with the blue rectangle is a painting with a yellow rectangle.
11. A purple rectangle and a yellow square are in the same painting.
8. Next to the painting with the yellow square is a painting with a green square.
3. The painting with the orange square is not next to the painting with the green square.
5. The painting with the blue square is on the right next to the painting with the orange square.

Parrots

At the zoo you can see parrots from different countries and in different colours.
These here are very colourful and seem to be from another planet. Read, colour and find out:

Which parrot has purple wings? ____________________

1. Between the parrot with the red body and the parrot with the orange body is a parrot with a green body.
2. One parrot has a blue head and a yellow beak.
3. Between the parrot with the orange tail and the parrot with a purple tail is a parrot with a red tail.
4. Next to the parrot with the yellow tail is a parrot with pink wings.
5. The parrot with the green beak is between the parrot with the yellow beak and the parrot with the blue beak.
6. One parrot has a yellow tail.
7. The parrot with the yellow head is between the parrot with the green head and the parrot with the pink head.
8. One parrot has an orange beak and a red body.
9. The parrot with blue wings is on the left next to the parrot with pink wings.
10. The parrot on the right has a green head.
11. One parrot has a pink body, red wings and an orange tail.

Parrots

At the zoo you can see parrots from different countries and in different colours.
These here are very colourful and seem to be from another planet. Read, colour and find out:

Which parrot has purple wings? ____________________

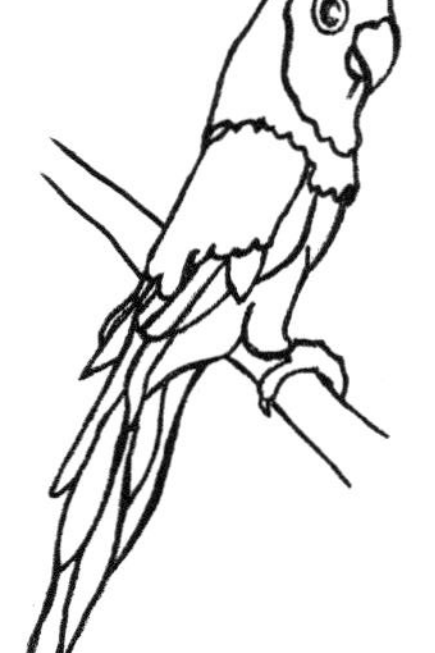

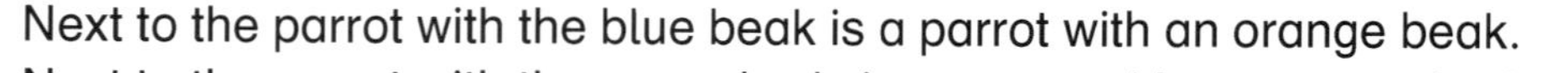

1. Next to the parrot with the blue beak is a parrot with an orange beak.
2. Next to the parrot with the green body is a parrot with an orange body and blue wings.
3. The parrot with a red tail is between the parrot with an orange tail and the parrot with a purple tail.
4. One parrot has a blue head and a yellow beak.
5. The parrot with the green head is between the parrot with the red head and the parrot with the yellow head.
6. One parrot has a pink body, red wings and an orange tail.
7. Between the parrot with a purple tail and the parrot with a blue tail and orange wings is a parrot with a yellow tail.
8. Between the parrot with the yellow beak and the parrot with the blue beak is a parrot with a green beak.
9. One parrot has a purple beak and a yellow body.
10. The parrot with pink wings is not next to the parrot with orange wings.
11. The parrot on the right has a red head.
12. The parrot with the red body is between the parrot with the yellow body and the parrot with the green body.
13. Next to the parrot with the yellow head is a parrot with a pink head.

Lösungen

Parrots

At the zoo you can see parrots from different countries and in different colours.
These here are very colourful and seem to be from another planet. Read, colour and find out:

Which parrot has purple wings? **Parrot 4**
Possible solution: 10/7/2/5/8/1/11/3/6/4/9

	parrot 1	parrot 2	parrot 3	parrot 4
head	blue	pink	yellow	green
beak	yellow	green	blue	orange
body	pink	orange	green	red
tail	orange	red	purple	yellow
wings	red	blue	pink	**purple**

10. The parrot on the right has a green head.
7. The parrot with the yellow head is between the parrot with the green head and the parrot with the pink head.
2. One parrot has a blue head and a yellow beak.
5. The parrot with the green beak is between the parrot with the yellow beak and the parrot with the blue beak.
8. One parrot has an orange beak and a red body.
1. Between the parrot with the red body and the parrot with the orange body is a parrot with a green body.
11. One parrot has a pink body, red wings and an orange tail.
3. Between the parrot with the orange tail and the parrot with a purple tail is a parrot with a red tail.
6. One parrot has a yellow tail.
4. Next to the parrot with the yellow tail is a parrot with pink wings.
9. The parrot with blue wings is on the left next to the parrot with pink wings.

Parrots

At the zoo you can see parrots from different countries and in different colours.
These here are very colourful and seem to be from another planet. Read, colour and find out:

Which parrot has purple wings? **Parrot 4**
Possible solution: 11/5/13/4/8/1/9/12/2/6/3/7/10

	parrot 1	parrot 2	parrot 3	parrot 4	parrot 5
head	blue	pink	yellow	green	red
beak	yellow	green	blue	orange	purple
body	pink	orange	green	red	yellow
tail	orange	red	purple	yellow	blue
wings	red	blue	pink	**purple**	orange

11. The parrot on the right has a red head.
5. The parrot with the green head is between the parrot with the red head and the parrot with the yellow head.
13. Next to the parrot with the yellow head is a parrot with a pink head.
4. One parrot has a blue head and a yellow beak.
8. Between the parrot with the yellow beak and the parrot with the blue beak is a parrot with a green beak.
1. Next to the parrot with the blue beak is a parrot with an orange beak.
9. One parrot has a purple beak and a yellow body.
12. The parrot with the red body is between the parrot with the yellow body and the parrot with the green body.
2. Next to the parrot with the green body is a parrot with an orange body and blue wings.
6. One parrot has a pink body, red wings and an orange tail.
3. The parrot with a red tail is between the parrot with an orange tail and the parrot with a purple tail.
7. Between the parrot with a purple tail and the parrot with a blue tail and orange wings is a parrot with a yellow tail.
10. The parrot with pink wings is not next to the parrot with orange wings.

Pizzas

A lot of people love pizzas. Which is your favourite?
Here are some children who eat their favourite pizza menus. The pizzas have two toppings each.
Read, fill in the pizzas (you can write the words or draw the toppings), and find out:

Who likes a shrimps and olives topping? ____________

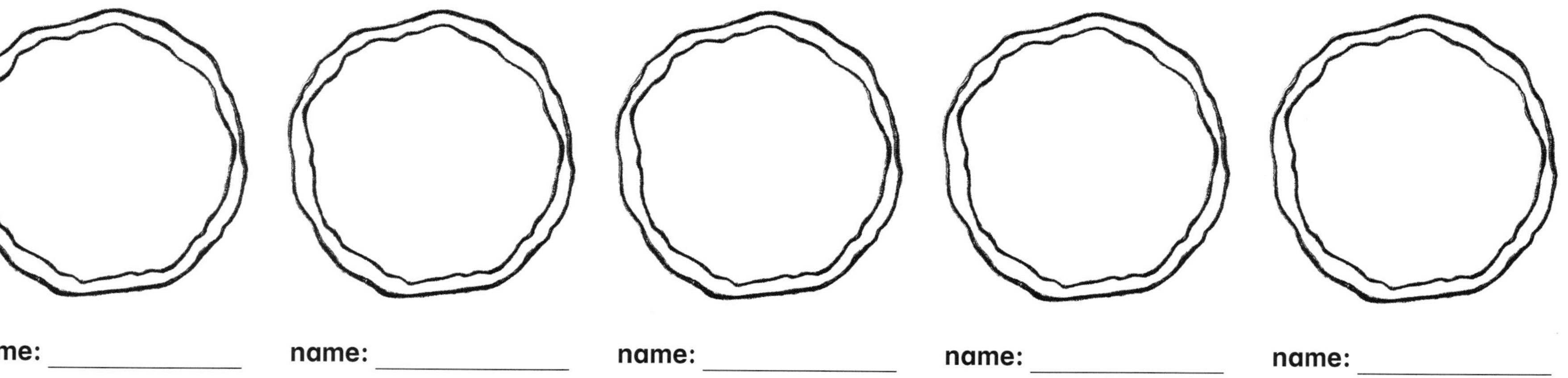

name: ________ **name:** ________ **name:** ________ **name:** ________ **name:** ________

1. Charlie is next to Ethan.
2. George is on the right.
3. Next to the child who likes a salami and mushroom topping is a child who likes ham and pineapples.
4. One girl likes a mushrooms and red pepper topping.
5. The child who drinks Fanta has a pizza with salami and mushrooms.
6. Next to the child who drinks apple juice is a child who drinks sprite.
7. Isabella is between George and Ethan.
8. Next to the child who drinks sprite is a child who drinks cola light.
9. The child who likes a broccoli and rocket topping is next to the child who likes ham and pineapples.
10. The child who drinks orange juice is next to the one who drinks cola light.
11. Amelia drinks apple juice.

Pizzas

A lot of people love pizzas. Which is your favourite?
Here are some children who eat their favourite pizza menus. The pizzas have two toppings each.
Read, fill in the pizzas (you can write the words or draw the toppings), and find out:

Who likes a shrimps and olives topping? ______________

name: ______ name: ______ name: ______ name: ______ name: ______ name: ______

1. Amelia drinks apple juice and likes a mushrooms and red pepper topping.
2. The child who drinks cola has a pizza with tuna and onions.
3. The child who likes a broccoli and rocket topping is next to the child who likes ham and pineapples.
4. Isabella is between George and Ethan.
5. Next to the child who drinks sprite is a child who drinks cola light.
6. One boy drinks Fanta.
7. The child who likes a ham and pineapple topping is next to the one who likes salami and mushrooms.
8. Next to the child who drinks apple juice is a child who drinks sprite.
9. Olivia is on the right.
10. Charlie is next to Ethan.
11. The child who drinks orange juice is next to the one who drinks cola light.
12. George is next to Olivia.
13. Next to the child who likes a tuna and onions topping is a child who likes salami and mushrooms.

Pizzas

A lot of people love pizzas. Which is your favourite?
Here are some children who eat their favourite pizza menus. The pizzas have two toppings each.
Read, fill in the pizzas (you can write the words or draw the toppings), and find out:

Who likes a shrimps and olives topping? **Charlie**
Possible solution: 2/7/1/11/6/8/10/5/3/9/4

name	Amelia	**Charlie**	Ethan	Isabella	George
pizza topping	mushrooms red pepper	**shrimps and olives**	broccoli rocket	ham pineapple	salami mushrooms
drink	apple juice	sprite	cola light	orange juice	Fanta

2. George is on the right.
7. Isabella is between George and Ethan.
1. Charlie is next to Ethan.
11. Amelia drinks apple juice.
6. Next to the child who drinks apple juice is a child who drinks sprite.
8. Next to the child who drinks sprite is a child who drinks cola light.
10. The child who drinks orange juice is next to the one who drinks cola light.
5. The child who drinks Fanta has a pizza with salami and mushrooms.
3. Next to the child who likes a salami and mushroom topping is a child who likes ham and pineapples.
9. The child who likes a broccoli and rocket topping is next to the child who likes ham and pineapples.
4. One girl likes a mushrooms and red pepper topping.

Pizzas

A lot of people love pizzas. Which is your favourite?
Here are some children who eat their favourite pizza menus. The pizzas have two toppings each.
Read, fill in the pizzas (you can write the words or draw the toppings), and find out:

Who likes a shrimps and olives topping? **Charlie**
Possible solution: 9/12/4/10/1/8/5/11/6/2/13/7/3

name	Amelia	**Charlie**	Ethan	Isabella	George	Olivia
pizza topping	mushrooms red pepper	**shrimps and olives**	broccoli rocket	ham pineapple	salami mushrooms	tuna onions
drink	apple juice	sprite	cola light	orange juice	Fanta	cola

9. Olivia is on the right.
12. George is next to Olivia.
4. Isabella is between George and Ethan.
10. Charlie is next to Ethan.
1. Amelia drinks apple juice and likes a mushrooms and red pepper topping.
8. Next to the child who drinks apple juice is a child who drinks sprite.
5. Next to the child who drinks sprite is a child who drinks cola light.
11. The child who drinks orange juice is next to the one who drinks cola light.
6. One boy drinks Fanta.
2. The child who drinks cola has a pizza with tuna and onions.
13. Next to the child who likes a tuna and onions topping is a child who likes salami and mushrooms.
7. The child who likes a ham and pineapple topping is next to the one who likes salami and mushrooms.
3. The child who likes a broccoli and rocket topping is next to the child who likes ham and pineapples.

Pocket money

Almost every child gets pocket money and tries to save it in order to buy something special. These children have piggy banks in different colours to save their pocket money which they get daily, weekly or monthly.
Read, fill in the information and find out:

Who gets £5? ____________________

name					
colour of piggy bank					
When?					
How much?					

1. One boy gets £1.
2. The purple piggy bank is next to the green piggy bank.
3. The child that gets pocket money monthly is next to the one that gets pocket money every two weeks.
4. Noah is between Isabelle and Archie.
5. The child that gets pocket money weekly is between the one that gets pocket money daily and the one that gets it every two weeks.
6. The yellow piggy bank is between the red and the green piggy bank.
7. The child that gets £25 is between the child that gets £20 and the one that gets £12.
8. The child with the blue piggy bank gets his pocket money daily.
9. Grace has a red piggy bank.
10. Jack is on the left and next to Isabelle.
11. One child gets £20 every three weeks.

Pocket money

Almost every child gets pocket money and tries to save it in order to buy something special. These children have piggy banks in different colours to save their pocket money which they get daily, weekly or monthly.
Read, fill in the information and find out:

Who gets £5? ____________________

name						
colour of piggy bank						
When?						
How much?						

1. The child that gets £12 is next to the one that gets £25.
2. One boy gets £1.
3. The child with the blue piggy bank gets his pocket money daily.
4. The child that gets pocket money monthly is between the one that gets it every two weeks and the one that gets it every three weeks.
5. Sophia has a pink piggy bank.
6. Noah is between Isabelle and Archie.
7. One child gets £10 every ten days.
8. The green piggy bank is between the yellow and the purple piggy bank.
9. The red piggy bank is between the pink and the yellow piggy bank.
10. The child that gets £20 is between the child that gets £10 and the one that gets £25.
11. Jack is on the left and next to Isabelle.
12. The child that gets pocket money weekly is between the one that gets it daily and the one that gets it every two weeks.
13. Grace is next to Archie.

Pocket money

Almost every child gets pocket money and tries to save it in order to buy something special. These children have piggy banks in different colours to save their pocket money which they get daily, weekly or monthly. Read, colour the piggy banks, fill in the information and find out:

Who gets £5? **Isabelle**
Possible solution: 10/4/9/6/2/8/5/3/11/7/1

name	Jack	**Isabelle**	Noah	Archie	Grace
colour of piggy bank	blue	purple	green	yellow	red
When?	daily	weekly	every two weeks	monthly	every three weeks
How much?	£1	**£5**	£12	£25	£20

10. Jack is on the left and next to Isabelle.
4. Noah is between Isabelle and Archie.
9. Grace has a red piggy bank.
6. The yellow piggy bank is between the red and the green piggy bank.
2. The purple piggy bank is next to the green piggy bank.
8. The child with the blue piggy bank gets his pocket money daily.
5. The child that gets pocket money weekly is between the one that gets pocket money daily and the one that gets it every two weeks.
3. The child that gets pocket money monthly is next to the one that gets pocket money every two weeks.
11. One child gets £20 every three weeks.
7. The child that gets £25 is between the child that gets £20 and the one that gets £12.
1. One boy gets £1.

Pocket money

Almost every child gets pocket money and tries to save it in order to buy something special. These children have piggy banks in different colours to save their pocket money which they get daily, weekly or monthly. Read, colour the piggy banks, fill in the information and find out:

Who gets £5? **Isabelle**
Possible solution: 11/6/13/5/9/8/3/12/4/7/10/1/2

name	Jack	**Isabelle**	Noah	Archie	Grace	Sophia
colour of piggy bank	blue	purple	green	yellow	red	pink
When?	daily	weekly	every two weeks	monthly	every three weeks	every ten days
How much?	£1	**£5**	£12	£25	£20	£ 10

11. Jack is on the left and next to Isabelle.
6. Noah is between Isabelle and Archie.
13. Grace is next to Archie.
5. Sophia has a pink piggy bank.
9. The red piggy bank is between the pink and the yellow piggy bank.
8. The green piggy bank is between the yellow and the purple piggy bank.
3. The child with the blue piggy bank gets his pocket money daily.
12. The child that gets pocket money weekly is between the one that gets it daily and the one that gets it every two weeks.
4. The child that gets pocket money monthly is between the one that gets it every two weeks and the one that gets it every three weeks.
7. One child gets £10 every ten days.
10. The child that gets £20 is between the child that gets £10 and the one that gets £25.
1. The child that gets £12 is next to the one that gets £25.
2. One boy gets £1.

Shopping summer clothes

Boys and girls like going shopping in various fashion shops. Here are five teenagers who go shopping for a new summer outfit. Read, fill in the shopping bags and find out:

Who goes shopping at Preckles? ________________

1. The teenager who buys blue shoes is next to the one who buys red shoes.
2. Between the teenager who buys a pink T-shirt and the one who buys a yellow T-shirt is a teenager who buys a black T-shirt.
3. The teenager who buys brown trousers is next to the one who buys grey shorts.
4. The teenager who goes shopping at Honey's is next to the one who goes shopping at Capland.
5. One girl goes shopping at Capland.
6. One teenager buys a white skirt and red shoes.
7. Bridget buys a pink T-shirt.
8. The teenager who buys grey shorts is next to the one who buys black jeans.
9. One boy buys brown shoes.
10. One teenager buys a red T-shirt and black jeans.
11. One teenager buys grey shoes and goes shopping at Mark's Place.

Shopping summer clothes

Boys and girls like going shopping in various fashion shops. Here are five teenagers who go shopping for a new summer outfit. Read, fill in the shopping bags and find out:

Who goes shopping at Preckles? ____________________

1. Bridget buys a pink T-shirt.
2. One teenager buys a white skirt and red shoes.
3. The teenager who goes shopping at Mark's Place is next to the one who goes shopping at Funworld.
4. One teenager buys a green T-shirt and blue jeans.
5. The teenager who goes shopping at Honey's is next to the one who goes shopping at Capland.
6. One teenager buys black shoes and goes shopping at Funworld.
7. One girl goes shopping at Capland.
8. Between the teenager who buys red shoes and the one who buys brown shoes is a teenager who buys blue shoes.
9. The teenager who buys brown trousers is next to the one who buys grey shorts.
10. Between the teenager who buys a pink T-shirt and the one who buys a yellow T-shirt is a teenager who buys a black T-shirt.
11. The teenager who buys grey shoes is next to the one who buys brown shoes.
12. The teenager who buys black jeans is between the one who buys blue jeans and the one who buys grey shorts.
13. One girl buys a red T-shirt.

Shopping summer clothes

Boys and girls like going shopping in various fashion shops. Here are five teenagers who go shopping for a new summer outfit. Read, fill in the shopping bags and find out:

Who goes shopping at Preckles? **Larry**
Possible solution: 7/2/10/8/3/6/1/9/11/5/4

	Sally	Larry	William	Bridget
T-shirt	red	yellow	black	pink
shoes	grey	brown	blue	red
shop	Mark's Place	**Preckles**	Honey's	Capland
trousers/jeans/skirt	black jeans	grey shorts	brown trousers	white skirt

7. Bridget buys a pink T-shirt.
2. Between the teenager who buys a pink T-shirt and the one who buys a yellow T-shirt is a teenager who buys a black T-shirt.
10. One teenager buys a red T-shirt and black jeans.
8. The teenager who buys grey shorts is next to the one who buys black jeans.
3. The teenager who buys brown trousers is next to the one who buys grey shorts.
6. One teenager buys a white skirt and red shoes.
1. The teenager who buys blue shoes is next to the one who buys red shoes.
9. One boy buys brown shoes.
11. One teenager buys grey shoes and goes shopping at Mark's Place.
5. One girl goes shopping at Capland.
4. The teenager who goes shopping at Honey's is next to the one who goes shopping at Capland.

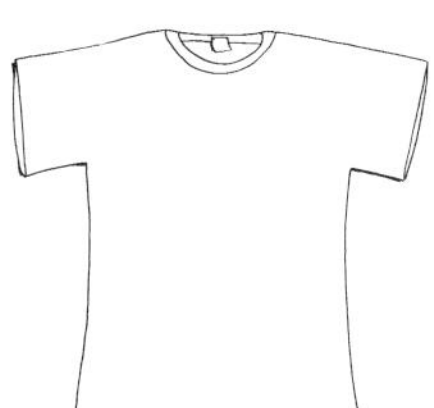

Shopping summer clothes

Boys and girls like going shopping in various fashion shops. Here are five teenagers who go shopping for a new summer outfit. Read, fill in the shopping bags and find out:

Who goes shopping at Preckles? **Larry**
Possible solution: 1/10/13/4/12/9/2/8/11/6/3/7/5

	Thomas	Sally	Larry	William	Bridget
T-shirt	green	red	yellow	black	pink
shoes	black	grey	brown	blue	red
shop	Funworld	Mark's Place	**Preckles**	Honey's	Capland
trousers/jeans/ skirt	blue jeans	black jeans	grey shorts	brown trousers	white skirt

1. Bridget buys a pink T-shirt.
10. Between the teenager who buys a pink T-shirt and the one who buys a yellow T-shirt is a teenager who buys a black T-shirt.
13. One girl buys a red T-shirt.
4. One teenager buys a green T-shirt and blue jeans.
12. The teenager who buys black jeans is between the one who buys blue jeans and the one who buys grey shorts.
9. The teenager who buys brown trousers is next to the one who buys grey shorts.
2. One teenager buys a white skirt and red shoes.
8. Between the teenager who buys red shoes and the one who buys brown shoes is a teenager who buys blue shoes.
11. The teenager who buys grey shoes is next to the one who buys brown shoes.
6. One teenager buys black shoes and goes shopping at Funworld.
3. The teenager who goes shopping at Mark's Place is next to the one who goes shopping at Woolworths.
7. One girl goes shopping at Capland.
5. The teenager who goes shopping at Honey's is next to the one who goes shopping at Capland.

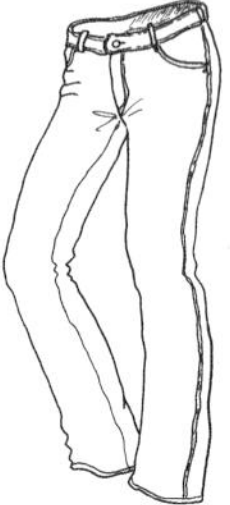

Shopping winter clothes

When winter comes most children need new clothes because they have grown over the summer. These children buy new winter clothes and check their outfit in the mirror. Read, colour the clothes and find out:

Who buys a blue woolly hat? ____________________

1. The child with the blue anorak is next to the one with the green anorak.
2. One child has orange trousers and black boots.
3. Between the child with a green scarf and the one with an orange scarf is a child with a red scarf.
4. One child has grey boots and a green scarf.
5. One child has a red anorak and yellow trousers.
6. One child has a blue scarf and a yellow woolly hat.
7. Between the child with black boots and the one with brown boots is a child with blue boots.
8. Next to the child with a brown woolly hat is a child with a purple woolly hat.
9. The child on the left has a brown anorak and is next to the child with the green anorak.
10. Between the child with yellow trousers and the one with red trousers is a child with grey trousers.
11. Next to the child with a yellow woolly hat is a child with a brown woolly hat.

Shopping winter clothes

When winter comes most children need new clothes because they have grown over the summer. These children buy new winter clothes and check their outfit in the mirror. Read, colour the clothes and find out:

Who buys a blue woolly hat? ____________________

1. Next to the child with grey trousers is a child with red trousers.
2. Between the child with a green scarf and the one with an orange scarf is a child with a red scarf.
3. The child on the left has a brown anorak and is next to the child with the green anorak.
4. Between the child with a yellow woolly hat and the one with a purple woolly hat is a child with a brown woolly hat.
5. Between the child with black boots and the child with brown boots is a child with blue boots.
6. One child has a grey anorak, blue trousers and red boots.
7. Next to the child with an orange scarf is a child with a blue scarf and a yellow woolly hat.
8. One child has grey boots and a green scarf.
9. Between the child with the blue trousers and the one with grey trousers is a child with yellow trousers.
10. The child with the blue anorak is between the one with the green anorak and the one with the red anorak.
11. One child has a yellow scarf.
12. The child with a green woolly hat is not next to the child with a purple woolly hat.
13. One child has orange trousers and black boots.

Lösungen

Shopping winter clothes

When winter comes most children need new clothes because they have grown over the summer. These children buy new winter clothes and check their outfit in the mirror. Read, colour the clothes and find out:

Who buys a blue woolly hat? **Millie**
Possible solution: 9/1/5/10/2/7/4/3/6/11/8

	Harry	Evelyn	Joshua	Millie
anorak	brown	green	blue	red
trousers	orange	red	grey	yellow
boots	black	blue	brown	grey
scarf	blue	orange	red	green
woolly hat	yellow	brown	purple	**blue**

9. The child on the left has a brown anorak and is next to the child with the green anorak.
1. The child with the blue anorak is next to the one with the green anorak.
5. One child has a red anorak and yellow trousers.
10. Between the child with yellow trousers and the one with red trousers is a child with grey trousers.
2. One child has orange trousers and black boots.
7. Between the child with black boots and the one with brown boots is a child with blue boots.
4. One child has grey boots and a green scarf.
3. Between the child with a green scarf and the one with an orange scarf is a child with a red scarf.
6. One child has a blue scarf and a yellow woolly hat.
11. Next to the child with a yellow woolly hat is a child with a brown woolly hat.
8. Next to the child with a brown woolly hat is a child with a purple woolly hat.

Shopping winter clothes

When winter comes most children need new clothes because they have grown over the summer. These children buy new winter clothes. Read, colour the clothes and find out:

Who buys a blue woolly hat? **Millie**
Possible solution: 3/10/6/9/1/13/5/8/2/7/11/4/12

	Harry	Evelyn	Joshua	Millie	Mohammed
anorak	brown	green	blue	red	grey
trousers	orange	red	grey	yellow	blue
boots	black	blue	brown	grey	red
scarf	blue	orange	red	green	yellow
woolly hat	yellow	brown	purple	**blue**	green

3. The child on the left has a brown anorak and is next to the child with the green anorak.
10. The child with the blue anorak is between the one with the green anorak and the one with the red anorak.
6. One child has a grey anorak, blue trousers and red boots.
9. Between the child with the blue trousers and the one with grey trousers is a child with yellow trousers.
1. Next to the child with grey trousers is a child with red trousers.
13. One child has orange trousers and black boots.
5. Between the child with black boots and the child with brown boots is a child with blue boots.
8. One child has grey boots and a green scarf.
2. Between the child with a green scarf and the one with an orange scarf is a child with a red scarf.
7. Next to the child with an orange scarf is a child with a blue scarf and a yellow woolly hat.
11. One child has a yellow scarf.
4. Between the child with a yellow woolly hat and the one with a purple woolly hat is a child with a brown woolly hat.
12. The child with a green woolly hat is not next to the child with a purple woolly hat.

Sights in the USA

There is a lot to see and explore in the United States of America.
These children spend their holidays in different states and visit the most famous sights.
Read, fill in the table and find out:

Who visits the Mount Rushmore National Memorial? ______________________

name					
month					
state					
sight					

1. Finley goes to the United States in July.
2. The child that goes to South Dakota is between the one that goes to New York and the one that goes to Nevada.
3. The child that visits the Golden Gate Bridge is between the one that visits the Walt Disney World Resort and the one that visits Las Vegas.
4. The child that goes to the United States in May is next to the one that goes in January.
5. Alexander is on the right and next to him is Logan.
6. The child that visits the Empire State Building is not next to the child that visits Las Vegas.
7. One child visits the Walt Disney World Resort in Florida.
8. The child that goes to the United States in February is between the one that goes in July and the one that goes in January.
9. Lola is between Logan and Alice.
10. The child that goes to California is next to the one that goes to Nevada.
11. One child goes to New York in March.

Sights in the USA

There is a lot to see and explore in the United States of America.
These children spend their holidays in different states and visit the most famous sights.
Read, fill in the table and find out:

Who visits the Mount Rushmore National Memorial? ______________________

name						
month						
state						
sight						

1. Sienna goes to the United States in April.
2. Alexander is on the right and next to him is Logan.
3. One child goes to New York in March.
4. The child that visits the Walt Disney World Resort is between the one that visits the Grand Canyon and the one that visits the Golden Gate Bridge.
5. The child that goes to California is between the one that goes to Nevada and the one that goes to Florida.
6. Next to the child that visits the Golden Gate Bridge is a child that visits Las Vegas.
7. Next to Alice is Finley.
8. The child that goes to the United States in January is between the one that goes in February and the one that goes in May.
9. The child that goes to South Dakota is between the one that goes to New York and the one that goes to Nevada.
10. The child that goes to the United States in July is between the one that goes in April and the one that goes in February.
11. One child visits the Grand Canyon in Arizona.
12. The child that visits the Empire State Building is not next to the child that visits Las Vegas.
13. Lola is between Logan and Alice.

Sights in the USA

There is a lot to see and explore in the United States of America.
These children spend their holidays in different states and visit the most famous sights.
Read, fill in the table and find out:

Who visits the Mount Rushmore National Memorial? **Logan**
Possible solution: 5/9/1/8/4/11/2/10/7/3/6

name	Finley	Alice	Lola	**Logan**	Alexander
month	July	February	January	May	March
state	Florida	California	Nevada	South Dakota	New York
sight	Walt Disney World Resort	Golden Gate Bridge	Las Vegas	**Mount Rushmore National Memorial**	Empire State Building

5. Alexander is on the right and next to him is Logan.
9. Lola is between Logan and Alice.
1. Finley goes to the United States in July.
8. The child that goes to the United States in February is between the one that goes in July and the one that goes in January.
4. The child that goes to the United States in May is next to the one that goes in January.
11. One child goes to New York in March.
2. The child that goes to South Dakota is between the one that goes to New York and the one that goes to Nevada.
10. The child that goes to California is next to the one that goes to Nevada.
7. One child visits the Walt Disney World Resort in Florida.
3. The child that visits the Golden Gate Bridge is between the one that visits the Walt Disney World Resort and the one that visits Las Vegas.
6. The child that visits the Empire State Building is not next to the child that visits Las Vegas.

Sights in the USA

There is a lot to see and explore in the United States of America.
These children spend their holidays in different states and visit the most famous sights.
Read, fill in the table and find out:

Who visits the Mount Rushmore National Memorial? **Logan**
Possible solution: 2/13/7/1/10/8/3/9/5/11/4/6/12

name	Sienna	Finley	Alice	Lola	**Logan**	Alexander
month	April	July	February	January	May	March
state	Arizona	Florida	California	Nevada	South Dakota	New York
sight	Grand Canyon	Walt Disney World Resort	Golden Gate Bridge	Las Vegas	**Mount Rushmore National Memorial**	Empire State Building

2. Alexander is on the right and next to him is Logan.
13. Lola is between Logan and Alice.
7. Next to Alice is Finley.
1. Sienna goes to the United States in April.
10. The child that goes to the United States in July is between the one that goes in April and the one that goes in February.
8. The child that goes to the United States in January is between the one that goes in February and the one that goes in May.
3. One child goes to New York in March.
9. The child that goes to South Dakota is between the one that goes to New York and the one that goes to Nevada.
5. The child that goes to California is between the one that goes to Nevada and the one that goes to Florida.
11. One child visits the Grand Canyon in Arizona.
4. The child that visits the Walt Disney World Resort is between the one that visits the Grand Canyon and the one that visits the Golden Gate Bridge.
6. Next to the child that visits the Golden Gate Bridge is a child that visits Las Vegas.
12. The child that visits the Empire State Building is not next to the child that visits Las Vegas.

Sports

Doing some sport is very good for your health. These kids have special training days. Some sports they like very much and still – there are sports they dislike.
Read, fill in the table and find out:

Who dislikes playing tennis? ____________________

name					
training					
likes					
dislikes					

1. Between the child who dislikes playing volleyball and the one who dislikes athletics is a child who dislikes cycling.
2. One child likes dancing and has training on Sunday.
3. The child whose training is on Wednesday is between the one whose training is on Saturday and the one whose training is on Monday.
4. Ella is on the right and next to her is Mia.
5. The child whose training is on Friday is next to the one whose training is on Monday.
6. One child likes gymnastics but dislikes playing volleyball.
7. William is between Mia and Leo.
8. Between the child who likes dancing and the one who likes playing football is a child who likes swimming.
9. The child who dislikes playing badminton is not next to the child who dislikes athletics.
10. Poppy's training is on Saturday.
11. The child who likes playing table tennis is next to the child who likes playing football.

Sports

Doing some sport is very good for your health. These kids have special training days. Some sports they like very much and still – there are sports they dislike. Read, fill in the table and find out:

Who dislikes playing tennis? ____________________

name						
training						
likes						
dislikes						

1. The child whose training is on Friday is between the one whose training is on Monday and the one whose training is on Sunday.
2. Joseph is on the right and next to him is Ella.
3. Poppy's training is on Saturday.
4. Between the child who likes playing basketball and the one who likes swimming is a child who likes dancing.
5. One child likes gymnastics but dislikes playing volleyball.
6. The child whose training is on Wednesday is between the one whose training is on Saturday and the one whose training is on Monday.
7. Between the child who likes swimming and the one who likes playing table tennis is a child who likes playing football.
8. One boy dislikes playing golf.
9. Mia is between Ella and William.
10. Leo is next to William.
11. Between the child who dislikes playing volleyball and the one who dislikes athletics is a child who dislikes cycling.
12. Next to the child who dislikes playing golf is a child who dislikes playing badminton.
13. One child likes playing basketball and has training on Thursday.

Lösungen

Sports

Doing some sport is very good for your health. These kids have special training days.
Some sports they like very much and still – there are sports they dislike.
Read, fill in the table and find out:

Who dislikes playing tennis? **Mia**
Possible solution: 4/7/10/3/5/2/8/11/6/1/9

name	Poppy	Leo	William	Mia	Ella
training	Saturday	Wednesday	Monday	Friday	Sunday
likes	gymnastics	playing table tennis	playing football	swimming	dancing
dislikes	playing volleyball	cycling	athletics	**playing tennis**	playing badminton

4. Ella is on the right and next to her is Mia.
7. William is between Mia and Leo.
10. Poppy's training is on Saturday.
3. The child whose training is on Wednesday is between the one whose training is on Saturday and the one whose training is on Monday.
5. The child whose training is on Friday is next to the one whose training is on Monday.
2. One child likes dancing and has training on Sunday.
8. Between the child who likes dancing and the one who likes playing football is a child who likes swimming.
11. The child who likes playing table tennis is next to the child who likes playing football.
6. One child likes gymnastics but dislikes playing volleyball.
1. Between the child who dislikes playing volleyball and the one who dislikes athletics is a child who dislikes cycling.
9. The child who dislikes playing badminton is not next to the child who dislikes athletics.

Sports

Doing some sport is very good for your health. These kids have special training days.
Some sports they like very much and still – there are sports they dislike.
Read, fill in the table and find out:

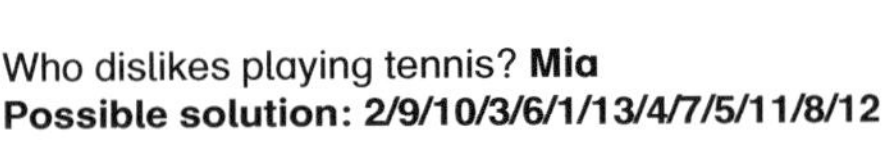

Who dislikes playing tennis? **Mia**
Possible solution: 2/9/10/3/6/1/13/4/7/5/11/8/12

name	Poppy	Leo	William	**Mia**	Ella	Joseph
training	Saturday	Wednesday	Monday	Friday	Sunday	Thursday
likes	gymnastics	playing table tennis	playing football	swimming	dancing	playing basketball
dislikes	playing volleyball	cycling	athletics	**playing tennis**	playing badminton	playing golf

2. Joseph is on the right and next to him is Ella.
9. Mia is between Ella and William.
10. Leo is next to William.
3. Poppy's training is on Saturday.
6. The child whose training is on Wednesday is between the one whose training is on Saturday and the one whose training is on Monday.
1. The child whose training is on Friday is between the one whose training is on Monday and the one whose training is on Sunday.
13. One child likes playing basketball and has training on Thursday.
4. Between the child who likes playing basketball and the one who likes swimming is a child who likes dancing.
7. Between the child who likes swimming and the one who likes playing table tennis is a child who likes playing football.
5. One child likes gymnastics but dislikes playing volleyball.
11. Between the child who dislikes playing volleyball and the one who dislikes athletics is a child who dislikes cycling.
8. One boy dislikes playing golf.
12. Next to the child who dislikes playing golf is a child who dislikes playing badminton.

US Presidents

There were 43 presidents of the United States so far. Barack Obama is the current president and really famous. But do you know anything of the other presidents? Read the sentences, fill in the table and find out:

Which president made cowboy films? It was ____________________

president				
age				
party				
presidential period				
special information				

1. The president on the right is John F. Kennedy.
2. Next to the president who became 56 years old is a president who became 93 years old.
3. Between the republican president and the president who had no party is another republican who was president from 1861–1865.
4. The president who was shot in Dallas is not next to the president who abolished slavery.
5. The president who became 46 years old was a Democrat and was president from 1961–1963.
6. Between John F. Kennedy and Abraham Lincoln is Ronald Reagan.
7. Next to the first president of the United States is the president who abolished slavery.
8. The Republican who was president from 1981–1989 is next to the president whose period ended in 1963.
9. George Washington became 67 years old.
10. The first president of the United States reigned from 1789–1797.
11. Next to the president who became 67 years old is a president who became 56 years old.

US Presidents

There were 43 presidents of the United States so far. Barack Obama is the current president and really famous. But do you know anything of the other presidents? Read the sentences, fill in the table and find out:

Which president made cowboy films? It was ______________________

president					
age					
party					
presidential period					
special information					

1. Franklin D. Roosevelt became 63 years old and was a Democrat.
2. Next to John F. Kennedy is Ronald Reagan.
3. The president on the right is John F. Kennedy.
4. The president who became 46 years old was a Democrat and was president from 1961–1963.
5. Next to the president who reigned till 1865 is a president who reigned from 1789–1797.
6. The president who was shot in Dallas is not next to the president who abolished slavery.
7. Between Ronald Reagan and George Washington is Abraham Lincoln.
8. The Republican president who became 56 years old is next to the one who became 67 years old.
9. Between the president who reigned until 1963 and the one who reigned from 1861-1865 is a president who reigned from 1981–1989.
10. Between the president with more than two presidential periods and the president who abolished slavery is the first president of the United States.
11. Next to the president who became 63 years old is a president who became 67 years old and belonged to no party.
12. The president who reigned from 1933–1945 was the only president with more than two periods.
13. The president who became 93 years old was a Republican and is next to the president who became 56 years old.

US Presidents

There were 43 presidents of the United States so far. Barack Obama is the current president and really famous. But do you know anything of the other presidents? Read the sentences, fill in the table and find out:

Which president made cowboy films? It was **Ronald Reagan**
Possible solution: 1/6/9/11/2/5/8/3/10/7/4

president	George Washington	Abraham Lincoln	**Ronald Reagan**	John F. Kennedy
age	67	56	93	46
party	no party	republican	republican	democrat
presidential period	1789–1797	1861–1865	1981–1989	1961–1963
special information	first president of the United States	abolished slavery	**made cowboy films**	was shot in Dallas

1. The president on the right is John F. Kennedy.
6. Between John F. Kennedy and Abraham Lincoln is Ronald Reagan.
9. George Washington became 67 years old.
11. Next to the president who became 67 years old is a president who became 56 years old.
2. Next to the president who became 56 years old is a president who became 93 years old.
5. The president who became 46 years old was a Democrat and was president from 1961–1963.
8. The Republican who was president from 1981–1989 is next to the president whose period ended in 1963.
3. Between the republican president and the president who had no party is another republican who was president from 1861–1865.
10. The first president of the United States reigned from 1789–1797.
7. Next to the first president of the United States is the president who abolished slavery.
4. The president who was shot in Dallas is not next to the president who abolished slavery.

US Presidents

There were 43 presidents of the United States so far. Barack Obama is the current president and really famous. But do you know anything of the other presidents? Read the sentences, fill in the table and find out:

Which president made cowboy films? It was **Ronald Reagan**
Possible solution: 3/2/7/1/11/8/13/4/9/5/12/10/6

president	Franklin D. Roosevelt	George Washington	Abraham Lincoln	**Ronald Reagan**	John F. Kennedy
age	63	67	56	93	46
party	democrat	no party	republican	republican	democrat
presidential period	1933–1945	1789–1797	1861–1865	1981–1989	1961–1963
special information	only president with more than 2 periods	first president of the United States	abolished slavery	**made cowboy films**	was shot in Dallas

3. The president on the right is John F. Kennedy.
2. Next to John F. Kennedy is Ronald Reagan.
7. Between Ronald Reagan and George Washington is Abraham Lincoln.
1. Franklin D. Roosevelt became 63 years old and was a Democrat.
11. Next to the president who became 63 years old is a president who became 67 years old and belonged to no party.
8. The Republican president who became 56 years old is next to the one who became 67 years old.
13. The president who became 93 years old was a Republican and is next to the president who became 56 years old.
4. The president who became 46 years old was a Democrat and was president from 1961–1963.
9. Between the president who reigned until 1963 and the one who reigned from 1861–1965 is a president who reigned from 1981–1989.
5. Next to the president who reigned till 1865 is a president who reigned from 1789–1797.
12. The president who reigned from 1933–1945 was the only president with more than two periods.
10. Between the president with more than two presidential periods and the president who abolished slavery is the first president of the United States.
6. The president who was shot in Dallas is not next to the president who abolished slavery.

Quellenverzeichnis

Bildquellen

Cover-Illustration:
Amerikanische Präsidenten ©Julia Flasche

Piktos:
Pikto ausmalen © Julia Flasche
Pikto Tabelle ausfüllen © Julia Flasche
Pikto zeichnen © Julia Flasche
Pikto easy © Julia Flasche
Pikto difficult © Julia Flasche

S. 5:
Basketballspieler © Daniela Bühnen

S. 8/9:
Alien © Kerrin Paulsen

S. 11–13:
Strand Harrison © Kerrin Paulsen
Strand Erin © Kerrin Paulsen
Strand Luke © Kerrin Paulsen
Strand Layla © Kerrin Paulsen
Strand Sophie © Kerrin Paulsen

S. 16:
Bananen © Fides Friedeberg
Brot © Julia Flasche

S. 17:
Wilhelm der Eroberer © Kerrin Paulsen

S. 18:
Richard Löwenherz © Kerrin Paulsen

S. 19:
Heinrich VIII. © Kerrin Paulsen
Elisabeth I. © Kerrin Paulsen

S. 23–25:
Handy © Mele Brink
Notebook © Julia Flasche

S. 26–28:
Schal © Katharina Reichert-Scarborough
Handtasche © Barbara Gerth

S. 29–31:
Sherlock Holmes © Kerrin Paulsen
Miss Marple © Kerrin Paulsen

S. 32–34:
Mädchen 1 © Kerrin Paulsen
Mädchen 2 © Kerrin Paulsen
Mädchen 3 © Kerrin Paulsen
Junge 1 © Kerrin Paulsen
Junge 2 © Kerrin Paulsen
Junge 3 © Kerrin Paulsen
Koch © Barbara Gerth
Zahnarzt © Barbara Gerth

S. 35–37:
Mädchen 1 © Kerrin Paulsen
Mädchen 2 © Kerrin Paulsen
Mädchen 3 © Kerrin Paulsen
Junge 1 © Kerrin Paulsen
Junge 2 © Kerrin Paulsen
Junge 3 © Kerrin Paulsen
Lehrerin an der Tafel © Mele Brink
Lehrer mit Schüler © Mele Brink

S. 38–40:
Blumenstrauß 1 © Kerrin Paulsen
Blumenstrauß 2 © Kerrin Paulsen

S. 42–44:
Fußball Junge 1 © Kerrin Paulsen
Fußball Junge 2 © Kerrin Paulsen
Fußball Junge 3 © Kerrin Paulsen
Fußball Mädchen 1 © Kerrin Paulsen
Fußball Mädchen 2 © Kerrin Paulsen

S. 44–46:
Mädchen 1 © Kerrin Paulsen
Mädchen 2 © Kerrin Paulsen
Mädchen 3 © Kerrin Paulsen
Junge 1 © Kerrin Paulsen
Junge 2 © Kerrin Paulsen
Junge 3 © Kerrin Paulsen

S. 47–49:
Kochen © Oliver Wetterauer
Spülmaschine © Natalie Meenen

S. 50–51:
Tisch © Kerrin Paulsen

S. 53–55:
Mädchen 1 © Kerrin Paulsen
Mädchen 2 © Kerrin Paulsen
Mädchen 3 © Kerrin Paulsen
Junge 1 © Kerrin Paulsen
Junge 2 © Kerrin Paulsen
Junge 3 © Kerrin Paulsen
Buckingham Palace © Stefan Lucas
Tower Bridge © Stefan Lucas

S. 56–58:
Bilderrahmen © Julia Flasche
Maler © Julia Flasche
Maler mit Staffelei © Julia Flasche

Quellenverzeichnis

S. 59–60:
Papagei 1 © Kerrin Paulsen
Papagei 2 © Kerrin Paulsen
Papagei © Julia Flasche

S. 62/63:
Pizza © Kerrin Paulsen

S. 64:
Pizza © Barbara Gerth
Pizzastück © Bert Breitenbach

S. 65–67:
Bargeld © Barbara Gerth
Sparschwein © Barbara Gerth

S. 68/69:
Einkaufstüte © Mele Brink

S. 70:
T-Shirt © Julia Flasche
Jeans © Marion El-Khalafawi

S. 71/72:
Winterkleidung Harry © Kerrin Paulsen
Winterkleidung Evelyn © Kerrin Paulsen
Winterkleidung Joshua © Kerrin Paulsen
Winterkleidung Millie © Kerrin Paulsen
Winterkleidung Mohammed © Kerrin Paulsen

S. 73:
Winterstiefel © Julia Flasche
Schal © Katharina Reichert-Scarborough

S. 74–76:
Mädchen 1 © Kerrin Paulsen
Mädchen 2 © Kerrin Paulsen
Mädchen 3 © Kerrin Paulsen
Junge 1 © Kerrin Paulsen
Junge 2 © Kerrin Paulsen
Junge 3 © Kerrin Paulsen
Golden Gate Bridge © Kerrin Paulsen
Mount Rushmore National Memorial © Kerrin Paulsen

S. 77–79:
Mädchen 1 © Kerrin Paulsen
Mädchen 2 © Kerrin Paulsen
Mädchen 3 © Kerrin Paulsen
Junge 1 © Kerrin Paulsen
Junge 2 © Kerrin Paulsen
Junge 3 © Kerrin Paulsen
Fußball spielen © Mele Brink
Basketball spielen © Mele Brink

S. 80–82:
Präsident Lincoln © Kerrin Paulsen
Präsident Kennedy © Kerrin Paulsen
Präsident Clinton © Kerrin Paulsen
Präsident Obama © Kerrin Paulsen
Präsident Roosevelt © Kerrin Paulsen
Präsident Washington © Kerrin Paulsen